WE KNEW JESUS

By

JOHN CALVIN REID, Ph.D., D.D.

*Minister of Mt. Lebanon Presbyterian Church,
Pittsburgh, Pennsylvania*

WM. B. EERDMANS PUBLISHING COMPANY

GRAND RAPIDS, MICHIGAN

WE KNEW JESUS
by John Calvin Reid
Copyright, 1954, by
Wm. B. Eerdmans Publishing Company

Set up and printed, January, 1954

PRINTED IN THE UNITED STATES OF AMERICA

We Knew Jesus

AFFECTIONATELY DEDICATED

To my father and mother

whose love for the Gospel and way of living it
awakened in me the desire to preach it.

INTRODUCTION

"The supreme lesson of life," Emerson once said, "is to learn what the centuries say about the hours."

This Series of "Impersonation" Sermons is my prayerful effort to discover and to declare what *eternity* says about the hours.

J. C. R.

Contents

1. *"I tried to kill Him"* — HEROD 11
   Matthew 2:3, 16

2. *"I provided the upper room"*
   — THE GOODMAN OF THE HOUSE 23
   A COMMUNION MESSAGE — Mark 14:13-15

3. *"I betrayed Him"* —JUDAS....................... 35
   Matthew 27:5

4. *"I denied Him"* — PETER 47
   Luke 22:61, 62

5. *"I was His closest friend"* — JOHN 59
   Mark 3:17

6. *"I condemned Him"* — CAIAPHAS 71
   John 11:49, 50

7. *"I sentenced Him"* —PILATE 83
   Matthew 27:22

8. *"I carried His cross"* — SIMON 93
   Mark 15:21 (ASV)

9. *"I was crucified with Him"*
   — THE ROBBER WHO REPENTED 103
   Luke 23:42, 43

10. *"I assisted at His burial"* — NICODEMUS 115
    John 19:39

11. *"I was His missionary"* — PAUL 127
    Philippians 3:13, 14 (RSV)

12. *"He raised me from the dead"* — LAZARUS 137
    AN EASTER MESSAGE — John 11:43, 44

ACKNOWLEDGMENT

A great deal of care has been taken to find copyrights and their owners, and it is my hope that credit has been given in every instance where the source of the material is known. If any materials have been used without proper acknowledgment, it is because careful search did not reveal the owners of the copyrights. If further information regarding copyrights and copyrighted material is obtained, proper acknowledgment will be made in future editions. Special thanks are due to the John Knox Press for permission to use one sermon (*I sentenced Him*) which is reprinted from my previous book, *On Toward the Goal*.

The Author

HEROD

"I tried to kill Him"

When Herod the king had heard these things, he was troubled, and all Jerusalem with him . . . Then Herod, when he saw that he was mocked of the wise men, was exceeding wroth, and sent forth, and slew all the children that were in Bethlehem, and in all the coasts thereof, from two years old and under . . . MATTHEW 2:3, 16

1

"I tried to kill Him"
—HEROD

MY NAME IS HEROD, known in my day as "Herod the Great," for I was the first and the most famous of the four Herods mentioned in your New Testament. I was king of Judaea when Jesus was born in Bethlehem, less than four miles from my palace in Jerusalem.

The news of His birth greatly troubled me, and I made a determined effort to kill Him when He was still an infant. The account of that attempted crime in Matthew, chapter two, is the only story about me in your Bible. I was past seventy at that time, in the last year of my reign. But for you to understand why I tried to murder the child Jesus, you must know something of my earlier years.

In my prime I was one of the world's most successful and notable men. Being a personal friend of both Antony and Augustus Caesar, it was my good fortune to be appointed governor of Galilee when I was only twenty-five years of age. Four years later Antony and Caesar introduced me to the Roman Senate where I made such a favorable impression that the Senate decreed that I should be king of Judaea. For over forty years I held that office, ruling the Jews from Jerusalem. In my palace I once entertained Cleopatra, queen of Egypt, even as Solomon before me had entertained the Queen of Sheba.

I was strong and victorious in war, wise in the ways of the world, shrewd in diplomacy, always managing to stay in favor with the powers that ruled in Rome. True, I made many enemies, but always I was able to outwit them or to kill them — (to me one plan was as good as the other!) — with just one exception, the one which the Gospel of Matthew records and about which I shall comment later.

During the time I was king in Jerusalem, I engaged in great building exploits. I rebuilt Samaria, renaming it Sebaste (Greek for Augusta) in honor of the emperor's wife. This name it bears to this day; and stately ruins, which some of you may have seen, still tell of the elegance with which I adorned it.

Twelve years I spent in rebuilding Strato's Tower and in creating an artificial harbor for large ships — an achievement considered by many to be impossible. To this new city I gave the name Caesarea in honor of the emperor. I rebuilt the temple of Apollo at Rhodes, added gymnasiums at Tripoli, Damascus and Ptolmais, theaters at Sidon, Damascus and Jerusalem. My crowning architectural achievement was the rebuilding of the Jewish temple at Jerusalem. Constructed of huge blocks of white marble, when completed this temple ranked among the wonders of the world, being even more glorious than the one built by Solomon.

This temple I built, frankly, not from any religious motive but as a matter of political expediency. Behind my pious pretext of being grateful to God and desiring to honor Him, I was simply indulging my own personal ambition, flattering the Jews, and consolidating my power. Shameless hypocrisy, you say! But have you never practiced the same subterfuge— engaging in religious activities with worldly gain in view?

"I tried to kill Him"

In my case it all worked like a charm—at least for a while it did.   At times I was amazed at my attainments.   Like Solomon before me, I could say of myself:

> *I made me great works; I builded me houses;*
> *I planted me vineyards: I made me gardens and*
> *parks: I gathered me also silver and gold,*
> *and the treasures of kings and of the provinces:*
> *So I was great, and increased more than all*
> *that were before me in Jerusalem: whatsoever*
> *mine eyes desired I kept not from them, I*
> *withheld not my heart from any joy . . .*
>
> Ecc. 2:4-10 ASV

Joy! That word now sounds strange to my ears. What does it mean anyway?   Once I thought I knew, but I must have forgotten.   At the beginning of my career I thought joy was synonmous with fame, honor, power, riches!   So, when the tempter of my soul showed me, then a young man, all the kingdoms of this world and the glory of them and said: "All these will I give thee, if thou wilt fall down and worship me," I agreed! My soul to gain the world, a small price to pay, I thought. Moral principles? Bah! I resolved to be clever, to use trickery, bribery, the sword—any expedient which might advance my purposes! Always with care, of course, always with calculated reserve!   I planned to keep an upper hand over possible adverse reactions!   But I would not concern myself unduly with questions of right and wrong.   "When in Rome do as the Romans do!"   Be realistic and practical! To win the world's prizes, use the world's methods! Such were the principles that guided both heart and hand in the early days of my career.   Looking back from this point I realize I forgot just one thing, *Conscience!*   Only to find that conscience would not forget me.   As one of your well-known poets[1] has expressed it:

---

1. Dunbar, *World's Great Library of Literature*, Vol. 28; Page 16902

Good-bye, I said to my conscience
Good-bye for aye and aye,
And I put her hands off harshly
And turned my face away.
And conscience smitten sorely,
Returned not from that day.

But a time came when my spirit
Grew weary of its pace.
I cried, "Come back, my conscience,
I long to see thy face."
But conscience answered, "I cannot,
Remorse sits in my place."

But at the beginning I did not have time to be bothered
by conscience. I was too busy planning and achieving
worldly success. I remember how I led my army on a stren-
uous 340 mile march from Samaria to the rescue of Antony,
who was sorely pressed at the time by Tigranes, king of Ar-
menia. Together we captured the city of Samosata, bringing
to an end the Parthian War. In gratitude for my timely aid,
Antony dispatched his army to assist me in capturing Jerusalem, where the Jews under Antigonus had fortified the
city against me. After a siege of five months the city was
taken, and in 37 B. C. my reign began. I was not yet thirty
years old. The kingdoms of this world were fast becoming
mine!

Confiscating the possessions of the wealthy men of the
city, I heaped together a great quantity of silver and gold for
Antony and other Roman friends. Then I ordered the execution of forty-five of the chief supporters of the rebellion.
Antigonus himself was slain by Antony at my request, a request I reinforced by sending him a large sum of money.
Bribery? Yes! That was the least of my worries then. I
was still on the way up!

"I tried to kill Him"

To be sure of controlling the priesthood in Jerusalem I sent for a friend of mine, an obscure priest in Babylon whose name was Ananelus, and appointed him high priest. A short while after, to please my wife, Mariamne, I revoked this appointment and gave the office to her brother Aristobulus. But Aristobulus proved to be too popular with the people. I feared he might aspire to be king. So one evening at a swimming party with some of my friends at Jericho, he was "accidentally" drowned. There were angry whispers to the effect that it was at my instigation that these friends of mine playfully plunged him under the water and held him down too long, but when it was seen how I wept beside his body, and what a magnificent funeral I ordered for him, including a costly sepulcher, the whispers grew quieter.

But my wife Mariamne suspected the truth, and never forgave me. She was the most beautiful woman my eyes had ever seen. I loved her with my whole soul, and her coldness drove me mad. One day in a fit of rage, because she continued to treat me with disdain and to accuse me of being her brother's murderer, I ordered her execution. No sooner was she dead than my conscience leaped into awful life, and I began to suffer inward tortures beyond the power of words to describe. My love for her seized upon me in such a painful manner as to appear like divine vengeance for taking away her life. I bethought myself of everything to divert my mind from thinking of her, contriving feasts and entertainments for that purpose, but nothing would suffice. I therefore laid aside the administration of public affairs, being so far conquered by my grief that I would order my servants to call for Mariamne as if she were still alive and could hear them.

About this time a pestilence broke out upon the people of Jerusalem, carrying away by death many of the citizens, among them several of my closest friends. This was interpreted by many as another judgment of God for what I had done to Mariamne, and I was distressed all the more. I betook myself to desert places; and there, under the pretense of hunting, bitterly reproached myself, wishing over and over that I were dead. Sometime later I began to have violent pains in my head, for which the medicines of my physicians brought no relief whatsoever. But the pain in my head was as nothing compared to the pain in my heart. That pain is still as fresh as though my crime had been committed only yesterday.

> *Oh, Mariamne! now for thee*
> *The heart for which thou bled'st is bleeding . .*
> *Oh, Mariamne! where art thou?*
> *Thou canst not hear my bitter pleading . . .*
>
> *And is she dead?—and did they dare*
> *Obey my frenzy's jealous raving?*
> *My wrath but doom'd my own dispair . . .*
> *She's gone, who shared my diadem . . .*
>
> *And mine's the guilt, and mine the hell,*
> *This bosom's desolation dooming;*
> *And I have earn'd those tortures well,*
> *Which unconsumed are still consuming!*[1]

Perhaps you are now beginning to understand my state of mind as I am introduced to you upon the pages of your New Testament. For thirty-two years I had lived without Mariamne but not without my remorseful memories. My heart had become a hell of torment and fear, my home a wilderness of loneliness, my whole existence a nightmare. As time went on, it seemed my enemies increased and I found it more necessary to rid myself of them. Anxiety haunted me continually, driving me to atrocious crimes in a vain effort to make myself secure. I came to distrust even my closest friends and suspected even the members of my family of

---

1. Herod's Lament, Byron

plotting against me. In my desperation which approached
hysteria I ordered those whom I suspected one after another
to be killed. Among those executed were my two sons by
Mariamne. Little wonder Caesar once said: It would be
safer to be Herod's pig (Greek 'hus') than his son (Greek
'huios').

The judgment of God was visited also upon my body. I
became afflicted with a loathsome, terribly painful and in-
curable internal disease—the malignancy known to you as
cancer. I suffered as though a fire burned within me.
Neither by day nor night could I find any relief. I knew I
was near death's door, but found it impossible to change my
habits of thought and action, because my greed, jealousy and
suspicion and my desire for worldly power still held me fast!

As the hour of my death drew nearer, realizing that the
nation would be relieved to hear I was gone, I conceived a
plan which, for its fiendish audacity, may stagger your mind
to believe. I summoned to Jerusalem the principal Jews
from every village in Palestine, as if to bestow upon them a
parting blessing. Once they stood before me, I ordered them
locked in the Hippodrome, then calling for my sister Salome
and her brother Alexas, I said to them secretly: "I shall die in
a little while, so great are my pains . . . . but what principally
troubles me is this, that I shall die without being lamented,
and without such mourning as men usually expect at a king's
death. My desire therefore is this: as soon as I am dead,
and before public announcement is made, you shall send soldiers to the Hippodrome and they shall put to the sword all
the Jews imprisoned there, that they may be buried at the
same time with me and that there may be a great and mem-
orable mourning at my funeral." With tears in my eyes I
begged them that they would thus see to it that there should
be a great lament at my funeral. Fortunately they had the
good sense not to execute my diabolical plot, but the guilt of
planning the crime is with me still.

Shortly after my interview with Salome and Alexas, I was seized with such violent internal pains that I attempted to stab myself with a knife with which I had been paring an apple. An attendant prevented me but not until the report had gone forth that I was dead. Antipater, my eldest son, at the time confined to prison by my orders, hearing the report, sought to bribe his jailer to set him free that he might at once seize the kingdom. Instead, the jailer informed me of Antipater's intention. Whereupon, though at death's door, I found strength to raise myself upon my elbow, and commanded that Antipater should be executed without further delay and buried without honor. It was my last recorded act. Five days later I followed Antipater to the land of the dead.

This world and its prizes look quite different to me, now that I see them in the light of eternity. I now see and testify that it were better to live and die, keeping one's integrity and honor, in poverty, than gaining the whole world to lose one's soul. Also, I now see and warn you that once one becomes entangled in worldly policies and compromises, with a second sin required to cover a first, a third to cover a second, and so on and on, it becomes increasingly difficult, not to say impossible, to break away. The fly caught in the spider's web is doomed if it delays to flee—so I was doomed, after a few years of practicing, "When in Rome do as the Romans do."

But clearest of all I see this: When those Wise Men from the East came to Jerusalem saying, "Where is He that is born King of the Jews?" and I did not go with them to Bethlehem to worship Him, I passed up my last opportunity to be saved. As I have already told you, I was past seventy at the time, in the last year of my reign. Every day the cancer was eating its way closer to my heart. "Go and search diligently for the child," I said to them, "and when ye have found him, bring me word again that I may come and worship Him also."

18

"I tried to kill Him"

But I did not mean it. I was speaking in deceit. In my jealous suspicious mind I was thinking, "Another plot against me, another usurper, another heart for my dagger!" Behind my pious words I hid my murderous purpose.

You know what happened next. The Wise Men did not return by way of Jerusalem. When I learned they had disobeyed me, I was furious with rage and sent forth a band of my soldiers with orders to put to death all the children, girls as well as boys, under two years of age in Bethlehem. My own death being so near, I did not live to hear that the Christ-child escaped the slaughter.

Regardless of how you may judge me for that horrible crime, you cannot but realize that I was behaving true to form. Also you must admit that there was a sense in which I acted upon a true impulse. There was not room in the world for both of us. He represented principles so utterly different from mine that His kingdom and mine could not possibly exist at the same time and place. Of necessity one of us had to destroy the other. This is still true. Men consumed by worldly ambition cannot long succeed unless somehow they get rid of the Christ-child. Thus in your generation one dictator found it necessary to try to rewrite the New Testament, while another found it expedient to celebrate his own birthday instead of Christmas!

But one cannot be rid of Him! He is from everlasting to everlasting, and of His kingdom there shall be no end. How clear that is to me now. In trying to rid myself of Him I was attempting the impossible.

And I might have submitted to Him. I might have surrendered my kingdom to Him. I might have knelt with the Wise Men and placed my crown beside their gold and frankincense and myrrh at His feet. Thus I might have found forgiveness and peace and salvation. Thus you may still find it.

19

For you—It is not too late
For you—Now is the accepted time,
Today is the day of salvation.
For me—"Of all sad words of tongue or pen,
The saddest are these:
'It might have been'."[1]

---

1. Maud Muller, Whittier

THE GOODMAN OF THE HOUSE

"I provided the upper room"

*And he sendeth forth two of his disciples, and
saith unto them, Go ye into the city, and there shall
meet you a man bearing a pitcher of water: follow
him. And wheresoever he shall go in, say ye to the
goodman of the house, The Master saith, Where is
the guest chamber, where I shall eat the passover
with my disciples? And he will show you a large
upper room furnished and prepared: there make
ready for us.* MARK 14:13-15

2   (A Communion Message)

"I provided the upper room"
—THE GOODMAN OF THE HOUSE

WHAT IS MY NAME? And wherefore do you ask? The
New Testament does not disclose it; why should I? Let me
continue to be known simply for what I did for Jesus. I lay
no claim to greatness or fame. I possessed no extraordinary
talent, nor was I ever confronted by any unusual opportunity. One of the more or less unpretentious and obscure
friends of Jesus, I nevertheless loved Him with a full heart
and counted it my highest joy to do for Him what I could.

Jesus, like every great leader of men, had His public and
intimate company of friends—the Twelve Disciples personally selected by Him and called to office as a president forms
his cabinet, as a commander appoints his generals, as a business executive selects his board of managers. With them
He travelled through Galilee, preached to the multitudes,
comforted the poor, and healed the sick. To them He gave
private instruction and issued special orders. They were
His college of Apostles, the officers of His church, the leaders of His cause.

But, as you read the Gospels, other figures emerge, like
pictures from shadowed corners in a gallery, like unsigned

23

letters in a biography, like initials in a dairy. There was the unnamed woman who slipped quietly into the house where He was being entertained at supper and anointed Him with the precious ointment. There was Simon of Cyrene of whom the only record is that he lifted the cross from His smarting, bleeding back and carried it to Calvary. There was the soldier who touched a sponge to His parched lips as He neared the end.

It is to this quiet group that I belong—and to which, no doubt, many of you belong. When or how you met Jesus does not matter—whether it was through the reading of a book, the hearing of a sermon, the entreaty of a friend, gazing upon a picture, listening to a sacred song—the important thing is that you were instantly and irresistibly attracted to Him. From the beginning there seemed to be a natural affinity between His soul and yours. The result has been over the years a genuine and deepening friendship, stirred by many a revelation, nourished by many an hour of communion, strengthened by many an experience of prayer and praise, until now you know that He and you belong to one another for time and eternity. You feel, as a poet of your own generation has expressed it,

> *The stars look up to God*
> *The stars look down on me*
> *The stars shine over the earth, and*
> *The stars shine over the sea.*
>
> *The stars will shine for a million years*
> *For a million years and a day*
> *But Christ and I will live and love*
> *When the stars have passed away.*

Looking backward over my earthly life, I see more clearly than ever, as the New Testament writers imply by their silence, that my name did not matter, or my address, or my occupation. What did matter was the one act of service I was privileged to perform in behalf of my Master and the spirit in which I rendered it. I did it, not to be remembered, but because I loved Him! That is the way it is told in the Gospels; that is the way I would have it still.

As the tomb of the Unknown Soldier in your nation's capital is a monument, not to one individual patriot but to all who loved their country to the point of giving the last full measure of their devotion; so, let my deed be a symbol of service rendered by Christ's humble followers in every generation who may not make the newspaper headlines, but whose names are not forgotten in God's book of eternal remembrance! And let my example be a perpetual reminder that one does not have to be great or gifted or famous to serve Him acceptably. If you possess the simple qualities of thoughtfulness and kindness, you qualify.

Have you considered the difference between dutifulness and thoughtfulness? Dutifulness waits for a spoken command. Thoughtfulness anticipates commands by divining the desires of the heart. Dutifulness goes the first mile because ordered to do so. Thoughtfulness goes the first mile unasked and the second likewise for love's sake. The dutiful son or daughter finishes the household tasks assigned, then hurries away to play. The thoughtful one stops to ask, "Mother, is there anything else I can do?" The dutiful husband is faithful to his wife, he provides her with an adequate allowance, he brings home the groceries as requested. The thoughtful husband goes beyond that and thrills her, at least occasionally, with some delightful surprise. Dutifulness is the cup of obedience filled to the brim. Thoughtfulness is the same cup running over.

Is your Christian service characterized by the extra that cheerfully goes beyond the call of duty? Obedience? Yes, of course! Christ expects, He commands that—"If ye love me, keep my commandments." But if you truly love Him, you will not stop there. Love always outruns duty.

I speak from experience. The deed which is recorded of me in the New Testament was not something I did in the line of duty. I did not wait to be elected to an office or appointed to a committee. I was not commanded by Jesus to do what I did, or even requested. I volunteered to do it, and I did it for love's sake.

It was during His last week in Jerusalem. While the rulers and chief priests were trying to ensnare Him in His talk, while gossips were arguing about His claims, while His disciples were wondering when His kingdom would appear and contending about who would be the greatest, I was turning over in my mind how I might befriend Him. I could not preach or debate. I could not dissuade His enemies from their evil purpose. I could not lead an army to His rescue. But it was clear that He was not seeking to escape the cross, and I was sure He was not afraid. What would help Him most as He faced His great ordeal?

Then it came to me—a place of retirement, a quiet retreat where he could be alone with His disciples and keep the Passover. "I will offer Him my home," I decided. "He shall have the choicest room in my house."

Could I ever forget the warm glow in His eyes when I told Him of my plan and invited Him to be my Passover guest with His disciples? For once He had been understood. For once one of the desires of His heart had been anticipated and was to be satisfied. We set a time and place where two of His disciples might meet one of my servants. We agreed upon a secret sign, "a man carrying a pitcher of water," so His enemies would not not know. Thus, in due time, on what turned out to be His last night, He was my guest, in the Upper Room of my house.

I can see it, as though it were yesterday—Jesus and His disciples reclining upon the couches which I had arranged around the table, John's head upon his Master's breast. I can still hear the tone of His voice as He took into His hand the bread my wife had prepared, "This is my body which is broken for you," and lifting the cup my hand had filled, "This cup is the New Covenant in my blood." Afterward there were other words not less tender and unforgettable: "Let not your heart be troubled, ye believe in God, believe also in me . . . I am the vine, ye are the branches . . . Abide in me and I in you . . . Father, I will that they also, whom thou hast given me, be with me where I am that they may behold my glory." Yes, all of those words, known to you as the final discourse of Jesus, recorded in John, chapters fourteen, fifteen, sixteen, and seventeen, including His great High Priestly Prayer, were spoken in the Upper Room of my house on the Thursday night of Passion Week.

I joined in the hymn which Jesus and His disciples sang as they prepared to go out to the Mount of Olives, said goodnight to them at the door, watched their figures disappear in the darkness, then turned to re-arrange the room. It was midnight, but I was in no mood to hurry. The presence of Jesus seemed still to linger upon the couch where He had reclined, upon the table His hand had touched, upon the cup His prayer had blessed.

Then suddenly it came over me. Joy and pride welled up within my heart at the thought! This room was holy ground! Here the Master had eaten His last Passover with His disciples. Here He had instituted the Lord's Supper. Here He had spoken the tenderest words that ever fell from His lips. No longer would this room be used for the common purposes of life. It would be kept for the Lord, if and when He should return, and for His friends.

It was only natural that His disciples should return to my house after His crucifixion and burial. I was waiting for them at the door and without a word, for I understood their feelings, I led them to the Upper Room. They knew they were welcome to stay as long as they wished. As they left one by one later, I told them to come often, for it would always be His room.

You are not surprised, then, when I tell you that it was to that room that the women came running, early the first day of the week, with the first news of the Resurrection. It was to that room that Cleopas and his companion rushed that same night, coming all the way from Emmaus to make known that the Lord had been revealed to them in the breaking of bread. It was there that the risen Lord appeared Himself a few moments later saying, "Peace be unto you. As the Father hath sent me, so send I you. Receive ye the Holy Spirit." It was there that He appeared a week later showing His hands and side to Thomas and saying, "Be not faithless but believing."

And that is not all! It was there, in my Upper Room, that the church of the New Testament was born with just one hundred and twenty members, among them the mother of Jesus. It was there that the disciples "tarried," as the Lord had commanded, until they should receive power. It was there that His promise was fulfilled and, after forty days, there came from Heaven a sound as of a rushing mighty wind and all were filled with the Holy Spirit.

Since that day many glorious cathedrals have been built to the honor of Jesus' name, but not one can compare in sacredness with the shrine where the first church met. At countless times and places believing men and women have observed the Holy Communion, but no celebration of that sacrament could be as holy as the first, which took place in my Upper Room.

Do not misunderstand me. I am not boasting, but deliberately trying to provoke you to a holy jealousy. For you must realize that there is a sense in which each one of you may do what I did. Still at various times and places, the Lord Christ would hold communion with His friends. Still the one appropriate provision for that holy tryst is a large upper room, furnished and prepared.

See to it, then, I beseech you, that you give Him a *large* room. At His birth there was no room for Him in the inn. Later He faced cold winds of hostility and rejection until one day He exclaimed, "The foxes have holes, and the birds of the air have nests, but the Son of man hath not where to lay his head." Tragedy of tragedies, there are still hearts and homes where He finds no welcome at all.

Then there are those who open the door a little way when He knocks, but keep Him standing on the outside while they argue about His claims. Others want Him to enter by the back door and to use the servants' quarters. Their interest is limited to what He may do for them.

But there are others, in whose company I trust you belong, whose primary interest is in what they can do for Him. They joyfully welcome Him to their best and largest room. To them He is chiefest among ten thousand, the one altogether lovely, the most honored of all guests that could ever visit their souls. Their whole house and all that they possess are placed instantly and unreservedly at His disposal. I beseech you, give Him a large room!

Also, I pray you, give Him an *upper* room. In ancient times and in oriental homes, the upper room was like a veranda or patio. Being on the roof, it was a secluded place, away from the noise and din of the street; an elevated place, open toward the stars and to the eternity that lies beyond; a cool place, where refreshing breezes gently fanned away the heat of the day, and the peace of night descended as quietly as the dew.

Is there such a room in your life, my friend? And is Jesus always welcome there? Has He been oft invited in words such as these?

> *'Mid all the traffic of the ways—*
> *Turmoils without, within—*
> *Make in my heart a quiet place,*
> *And come and dwell therein;*
>
> *A little shrine of quietness,*
> *All sacred to Thyself,*
> *Where Thou shalt all my soul possess,*
> *And I may find myself;*
>
> *A little shelter from life's stress,*
> *Where I may lay me prone,*
> *And bare my soul in loneliness,*
> *And know as I am known;*
>
> *A little place of mystic grace,*
> *Of self and sin swept bare,*
> *Where I may look upon Thy face,*
> *And talk with Thee in prayer.*
>
> —John Oxenham

Once more, may I remind you to give Him a *furnished* room. In my upper room, I provided a pitcher of clean cool water at the door. Beside it were fresh towels and a basin. Inside was a table upon which I had placed the food and drink required for the Passover feast. Around the table were couches upon which Jesus and His disciples might recline in comfort as they ate the Passover and communed with one another.

My room was not furnished lavishly, but I did furnish it adequately and in good taste, keeping in mind all the while what would be acceptable and pleasing to Jesus. That is all He expects of anyone.

What is the room of your heart like on the inside? Is it characterized by attitudes and emotions in harmony with His

spirit? Is that mind in you which was also in Christ Jesus?
Has all bitterness and wrath and anger and clamor and slan-
der been put away from you with all malice; and are you
kind to one another, tender hearted, forgiving one another, as
God in Christ forgave you? Your room, thus furnished and
adorned, can not but be pleasing to Him.

And is your room ready *now*? When the disciples called
at my door, they were not told to wait. I did not straightway
begin to make excuses. They did not hear me say, "Oh, yes,
I did intend to provide a room for Jesus; in fact, I meant to
give Him my very best room. But it is not ready yet. I have
neglected to put it in order. Tomorrow it will be ready." But
tomorrow He was on the cross! Tomorrow would have been
too late! What folly if I had procrastinated! But I did not!
When His disciples arrived saying, "The Master saith, 'Where
is the guest chamber, where I shall eat the Passover with my
disciples?' " my room was waiting. *It was a large room. It
was an upper room. It was furnished. And it was ready!*

There was one thing He said that night in my house that
seemed to have been meant for me in particular, for somehow
I had the feeling that He was thinking of me as He spoke:
"In my Father's house are many rooms . . . I go to prepare a
place for you . . . and I will come again and will take you to
myself that where I am there you may be also." (John 14:1-3,
R. S. V.)

It was as if He had said: "I am your guest tonight, but one
of these days the tables will be turned—you will be my guest!
You have prepared for me this room; I, in turn, am going to
prepare an Upper Room for you. When it is ready, I, myself,
will come to invite you and to take you to live with me and my
friends in my Father's house forever."

He kept that promise, and so supreme has been my happiness since the day He took me to be with Him that it seems
as though it began only yesterday. In that heavenly home,
which He still calls His Father's house, there are many more

31

rooms prepared for other friends of His. Some are occupied; others are waiting, furnished and ready.

If you are His true friend, there will, of course, be one for you. As for the kind of room it will be, that will depend, will it not? upon the kind of room you provide Him here. So, once again, I beseech you, open wide the door of your heart and give Him a large upper room, furnished and ready.[1]

1. The author gratefully acknowledges his indebtedness to *The Upper Room* by John Watson

JUDAS

"I betrayed Him"

And he cast down the pieces of silver in the temple, and departed, and went and hanged himself.

MATTHEW 27:5

3

"I betrayed Him"
—JUDAS

I AM JUDAS ISCARIOT! Why do you shudder at the mention of my name? And why have none of you named your sons after me, as has been done in the case of others of the Apostles? It is a good name, or was, when it was given to me.

"Judas" means "praise of God." It reminds me, as it will you, how my parents rejoiced when I was born and gave thanks to God. One of the eleven sons of Jacob bore my name. So also did one of the brothers of Jesus—the one who wrote the book of Jude in your New Testament. So also did one of the most famous military leaders in Jewish history, Judas Maccabaeus. Just a few generations before mine he successfully led my people in a revolt against their conquerors, the Greeks, thereby winning for them for a brief time their national independence. Judas Maccabaeus was to us Jews in the first century what George Washington is to you Americans today, and I was named for him! Of course, I was proud of my name!

"Iscariot" means "son of Kerioth" or "citizen of Kerioth," signifying that I was from Kerioth, a small village several miles south of Jerusalem, in the region where the prophet Amos was born. I was the only one of the twelve disciples of Jesus to come from Judea. The other eleven were from Galilee. They did not have to go far to follow Him, for His ministry until the last week, was in Galilee. I left all for His sake, including my home fifty miles away.

So, you see, I made a good start. I was reared in a religious home where I was taught to believe in and to honor God, to love my country and people. Quite naturally, then, I considered it the greatest day of my life when I met Jesus of Nazareth and heard Him say, "Judas, follow me."

You do not understand why He chose a man such as I to be an Apostle? For the same reason that He chose Peter, James, John, and the others. Because at that time I was a man of promise and possibility. I was possessed of lofty ideals and noble purposes. I felt a genuine enthusiasm for Jesus and for His cause.

For over a year I lived with Him. I heard all His sermons. I witnessed His miracles. I preached His gospel. I listened to His prayers. I started on the road which leads straight to heaven, —but!

A well-known minister of your generation has called me, "The man who might have been." "There is a butterfly," he says, "a glorious winged creature, hidden away potentially beneath the repulsive exterior of the crawling caterpillar. But the caterpillars do not all become butterflies. The scientist tells us that a fly sometimes thrusts into the body of the caterpillar a tiny egg. The egg hatches into a grub which feeds upon the butterfly—forming elements in the makeup of that caterpillar. The caterpillar suffers no pain and does not feel that anything is amiss. It goes right on eating and growing and living its life as a worm, but its wings do not appear. The grub has destroyed its capacity of advance. The glorious winged creature which might have been is gone—it never becomes a butterfly."[1]

Shall I tell you what was the grub which kept me from becoming the man I might have been? It was *worldly ambition.*

As I have already told you, my parents gave me an illustrious name, a name associated in the annals of my people

1. Dr. Charles R. Brown

with patriotism, with power, with freedom. I was already an ardent enthusiast for the cause of Jewish independence when I met Jesus of Nazareth. That is why I cast my lot with Him. He was fearless. He was popular. He had the qualities of a leader. He seemed to be the answer to the dreams and hopes of our nation, writhing under the heel of the Roman conqueror. I was ready to follow Him, to fight by His side, to die for Him. Indeed I was!

So I was overjoyed, as were the other eleven disciples, when one day He announced to us secretly that He was the Messiah. That, as I now know, at that time meant one thing to Him, quite another thing to us. To Jesus it meant suffering; to us, dominion. To Jesus, a cross; to us, a sword and a crown. Eventually the others came around to His viewpoint, but not I! If His kingdom did not include earthly power, glory and honor, His cause was not for me!

Up until almost the end I kept hoping that He would see it my way and become a true son of David—a leader such as David was, or Solomon, or my namesake Judas Maccabaeus. My hopes took on fresh life when I witnessed what is known to you as the Triumphal Entry—Jesus riding into Jerusalem in the midst of a wave of Messianic enthusiasm as the multitudes shouted "Hozanna" and spread palm branches in front of Him. I was even more pleased as I watched Him cleanse the temple single-handed, overturning the tables of the money-changers and driving them out. This was the kind of Messiah I wanted—one who would use His right arm! Only I wanted Him to use it against Rome too! Things were beginning to move at last, and in the right direction! But only for a day!

The straw that broke the camel's back, so far as my patience was concerned, came a few nights later at the house of Simon the leper. As Jesus sat at the table following the evening meal, "There came a woman having an alabaster cruse of ointment, pure and very costly; and she brake the cruse and poured it over his head." If you will recall what an "anointing" signified to kings and prophets in the old Testament, you will understand what this woman meant by this act. She, like myself, was a Messianic enthusiast. She, as was the case with me, wanted to see Him move forward to mighty triumph as "God's anointed." Hers was a grand and lavish gesture designed to urge Him in the same direction that I wanted Him to take—toward His throne, toward the using of His power to deliver us from the hated Romans!

But in a flash, Jesus quietly turned the meaning of that act in a totally different direction. "She hath anointed my body beforehand for the burying," He said. No one was more amazed by these words than the woman herself. She had intended to point Him toward His crown, not His coffin!

But I was not amazed. By this time it had become an old story to me—Jesus turning away from earthly authority and power toward a cross! I was fed up with it! The game was up so far as I was concerned. No more of my ambitious life would I waste in a cause hourly approaching bankruptcy. The ship was sinking. It was time to get off, and to take what I could out of the wreck—revenge at any rate, and a little money on the side, thirty pieces of silver, but chiefly the gratification of my resentment against one who had disappointed my worldly hopes.

"Revenge is sweet?" Is there one here who believes that? I had my revenge, did I not? That is why I chose a kiss as the sign by which to point Him out to His enemies. To my disillusioned, vindictive spirit, I thought that kiss would be sweet. But I was tasting the bitterest gall when He turned His tender eyes upon me and said: "Friend, wherefore art thou come, betrayest thou the Son of man with a kiss?"

Are there those of you perhaps nursing in your heart, as I once did, feelings of spite, resentment and vengeance under

the illusion that revenge is sweet? Think again! Consider
what one of your own poets[1] has said:

O laddie, my laddie, with quick-flashing eye,
With boyish cheek crimson and pulse beating high,
You say you'll get even, no matter how long
It takes you to pay for a slight or a wrong.

But tell me, O laddie, just whisper it low,
The secret I long have been wanting to know;
When after your hurry and flurry and fret,
At last you get even, JUST WHAT DO YOU GET?

Is it something that gives you a glad thrill of joy,
That makes you a better, a manlier boy?
Is it something that conscience may whisper, 'Well done,'
And bring you sweet peace at the set of the sun?

O laddie, the whole world is waiting to know
The secret that puzzled wise men long ago;
If, after your worry and flurry and fret,
At last you get even, JUST WHAT DO YOU GET?

But vengeance was not the beginning of my sin. Vengeance was the final fruit. The beginning was *ambition*. I
wanted the good things of this life for myself and for my nation. My hopes were not all selfish, but neither were they
ever surrendered to the will and purpose of Jesus. The ambitions of John were worldly too at the beginning. Do you
remember how he and his brother requested a throne each
at the side of Christ in His kingdom? But eventually John
surrendered his ambitions and yielded his will to Him whom
he called Master. That I never did, and that was the ultimate difference between the two of us.

There is a legend, with which you may be familiar, to the
effect that a famous artist once planned to paint The Last
Supper. He selected his models with the greatest care. For

1. Florence Jones Hadley, quoted by Dr. Robert B. Whyte in *The
Sins That Crucified Him*, page 46

the Apostle John he found a young man who was strikingly handsome, with a look of high purpose and spiritual expression written across his countenance as if by the finger of God.

The artist left me until the last, and, seeking a model for a traitor, went to the lowest quarters of the city where criminals were bred. One day in a back street he chanced upon a man whose furtive look, whose hard, unsympathetic face and sordid expression met all his requirements.

For "a few pieces of silver" the man came and proved to be a most cooperative model. One day the artist noticed that his attention was fixed upon the face of John. "You like that face?" the artist inquired. And the man answered, "Yes, it was once my own." He was the same man who five years before had sat as the model for the portrait of John.[1]

At heart that legend is profoundly true. I might have been a John! He and I lived at the same time, walked under the same starlit Syrian sky, experienced the same temptations, fellowshipped with the same radiant Personality, shared the same Apostleship. Such a man as John I might have been, had I only surrendered my worldly hopes and ambitions to Jesus, as He challenged all of us to do when He said (how these words still ring in my ears!): "If any man will come after me, let him deny himself, and take up his cross, and follow me."

Or if not a John, I might have been a Simon Peter. My sin, base as it was, was not unforgiveable. There are those who have pointed out that I sinned against the most wonderful Person that the world has ever known, as if that made my case more hopeless. Just the opposite is true. I sinned against One who forgave as never man forgave. He forgave the adulteress, He forgave the robber who repented beside Him on the cross, He forgave Peter who denied Him. Never did He refuse forgiveness to anyone who sought it. He would have

---

1. I am indebted for this illustration to Dr. Charles R. Brown

forgiven me had I repented. Was He not telling me as much in the garden when with my traitorous kiss still hot upon His cheek He said, "Friend, wherefore art thou come?" He called me "Friend!" When He saw me at my worst, He did not denounce me. He still loved me and spoke tenderly to me. It was the last name by which He ever addressed me—"Friend!"

Why did I not repent? Perhaps for the same reason you are still carrying some burden of unforgiven sin upon your conscience. Repentance requires humility, self-abasement, a change of mind and heart, a willingness to turn around and to face resolutely in the opposite direction. The hardest thing a man ever does is to repent.

Repentence is far more than feeling sorry for sin, more than an inner loathing and the excitement of a terrified conscience. It is even more than confession. I confessed—"I have sinned in that I betrayed innocent blood." But I was speaking to men, not to God. I was speaking to my companions in crime—miserable comforters!—not to my Saviour. My cry was earthward not heavenward.

O that I had found it in me in that dark moment to flee to Christ. O that I had rushed to Him wherever He was to be found — in the court of the high priest, in the judgment hall of Pilate, to the cross—that breaking through all obstacles I had flung myself at His feet! What if the soldiers had cut me down. Then I had been the martyr of penitence and that very day would have passed with Him into Paradise!

Fundamentally, there was little difference between Simon Peter's sin that night and mine. The difference is in what we did afterward. We were standing at the same crossroads. He took the road to the right which led back to Him who came into the world to save sinners and who could say as none other has ever said, "Come unto me all ye that labor and are heavy laden, and I will give you rest." I took the other road, the road to the left, the road that led away from Jesus—to a tree in the valley and a rope and a leap into the darkness.

"Praise of God" was the name my mother hopefully gave me when I was born. Instead through all succeeding generations I have been the "Warning of God." It is in that role that I appear before you at this moment.

I would warn you that a good start is not enough.

Alcibiades, the infamous Greek who betrayed Athens to her enemies, was in his youth an ardent admirer and devoted disciple of Socrates whose life he once saved in battle. Robespierre, the evil genius of the French Revolution who remorselessly sent thousands of innocent people to the guillotine, in his younger days resigned his office of provincial judge because he could not conscientiously condemn to death any human being. Benedict Arnold, the most execrated of American traitors, once enjoyed the fervent friendship and confidence of George Washington. A good start, as my life unforgettably reminds you, if it is to count in eternity's final reckoning, must be tied in with a good ending.

I would warn you against being carried away by worldly ambition.

For all that is in the world, the lust of the flesh, and the lust of the eyes, and the pride of life . . . passeth away . . . only he that doeth the will of God abides forever. Therefore, what shall it profit a man if he gain thirty pieces of silver, or the whole world, and lose his own soul?

I would warn you against the bitter emptiness of revenge.

When the winds and waves of vengeful passion rush in upon your soul, do what we disciples once did when a sudden tempest struck our little boat. Call to Him who has power to say to angry seas and to angry hearts, "Peace be still."

"I betrayed Him"

I would warn you most urgently of all against the folly of impenitence.

It is not sinning that ruined me, and that may ruin you, but sinning and not seeking forgiveness! The sin which carried my soul to hell was not treason but impenitence. In the final analysis that is the only sin that carries any soul to hell —the sin of failing to repent! There is but one unpardonable sin, and that is the sin of failing to ask pardon!

So, remember, ere it is too late, there is a road other than the one I took when remorse stabbed my conscience wide awake. I point you to the road the awakened prodigal took when he came to himself in the far country and said, "I will arise and go to my father and will say unto him, Father, I have sinned against heaven and in thy sight." That is the road, the only road, that leads home. And it is never closed— neither by day nor by night.

Of these things, I, Judas, remind and warn you, lest you come to my place of torment. Instead, may your prayer be:

> *Before the cross of Him who died,*
> *Behold I prostrate fall;*
> *Let every sin be crucified.*
> *Let Christ be all in all.*
>
> *Let every thought and work and word,*
> *To Thee be ever given;*
> *Then life shall be thy service, Lord,*
> *And death the gate of heaven.*

PETER

"I denied Him"

And the Lord turned, and looked upon Peter. And Peter remembered the word of the Lord, how he had said unto him, Before the cock crow, thou shalt deny me trice. And Peter went out, and wept bitterly. LUKE 22:61,62

4

"I denied Him"

—PETER

I AM A MAN WITH TWO NAMES, SIMON PETER. My first name represents the man I was before I knew Jesus. My second name, Peter, "the Rock," represents the man I finally became because of what He meant to me and what He did for me.

I was anything but a man of rocklike qualities when first I began to follow Him. I was profane, impetuous, unstable. I have often marvelled that He ever chose me to be a disciple at all.

Yet this I know: From the hour He said, "Follow me," I belonged to Him. I must have disappointed Him many times. I failed Him utterly in the dark hour of His trial; but throughout, my heart was His.

That was one difference between me and Judas. Judas was false, he was insincere, a traitor. I was weak, but never a hypocrite I sinned deeply against my Lord, but I never ceased to love Him, nor did He ever cease loving me. That was what saved me in the end. In His heart and also, as I shall never forget, in His eyes was a love that would not let me go.

The story of my shameful denial is well-known to you, but my downfall was not as sudden as is generally supposed.

My profanity, for example, there was nothing sudden about that. It was the backwash of my sinful past, the resurrection of an old habit of bygone days when I was a fisherman on the lake of Galilee.

The lesson for you is that old habits of sin are hard to kill. No matter how long you may have followed Christ, the evil which was a part of you before you knew Him is buried in the depths of your subconscious, waiting for an opportunity to leap forth and to express itself in some new and awful form. This is the penalty for days given to sin. The man who has been a drunkard, an adulterer, a liar, or a user of profanity will always have to keep careful watch over the graveyard of his past.

Remember this too, you who are careless about your speech —when I wanted to convince others that I did not know Christ, I could not do better than to take to cursing. They did not credit my statements concerning Jesus; but they could not help believing my profanity. Profanity is still quite convincing evidence that one either does not belong to or has turned his back upon Christ.

Another factor which contributed to my fall was my failure to watch and pray in the garden of Gethsemane.

You will recall the serene courage of Jesus as He stepped forward to meet His enemies when they came to arrest Him, contrasted with our panic as we, His disciples, all forsook Him and fled. That contrast is accounted for at least in part by this: While He was praying we had been sleeping! Had I myself only stayed awake and prayed with Him in the garden, I had never denied Him in the courtyard!

How is it with you and your temptations? Are they proving too much for you? One defeat after another with seldom a victory? Could the trouble be that your prayer life is being neglected? You do not put on the armour of God as you begin the day, and later the enemy of your soul catches you unprepared. You do not keep your lamp filled with oil, so at times your light burns dim. We are at the heart of the trouble, are we not?—You need to heed, as I unfortunately failed to do, the Master's command as He entered the garden of prayer: "Watch and pray that ye enter not into temptation."

I made a third mistake later. After I entered the high priest's palace, I fell in with the wrong crowd.

You will recall that John was known to the high priest, and so had been admitted when Jesus was led in. Later he came back and spoke to the maid who kept the door, whereupon I also was allowed to enter. After that, John moved on in to where Jesus was and stood beside Him at His trial. Would that I had done that! But of me it is written that I "followed afar off." Which means that I remained for awhile in the shadows near the door, then later, as I began to feel the chill of the night, strolled forward and joined a group of the servants of the high priest and his officers who had kindled a fire in the yard.

These were my Lord's enemies as I well knew. The air was ringing with jest and laughter and profanity about Jesus—as I approached, but I did not object. I just tried to look as much like one of the scorners as possible without saying anything. But not to confess Christ in such a situation was, of course, just one step short of denying Him.

It is always dangerous for a follower of Christ to take his place among Christ's enemies without letting it be known who he is. "Blessed is the man that walketh not in the counsel of the ungodly, nor standeth in the way of sinners, nor sitteth in the seat of the scornful."

I had forgotten that. I had not yet learned the lesson which the Apostle Paul later underscored when he wrote to the Christians at Corinth: "Do not be deceived: 'Bad company corrupts good morals,'" That lesson I learned the hard way, after it was too late. For that reason I am earnestly trying to teach it to you before it is too late. Had I only stayed with John, my friend and His disciple, instead of falling in with those who made light of Jesus and scoffed at His claims, I had never denied Him!

Well, there you have it, the shameful story of my fall and the factors that contributed to it. Step by step closer and closer to danger I moved until at last I found myself cornered, cornered and goaded by the embarrassing questions of my ill-chosen companions, until in rage, terror and shame I lost all control, and adding to my three-fold denial oaths and curses, I cried, "I do not even know the fellow!"

Then suddenly, out of the darkness of the night, loud and clear, I heard a cock crow! Almost at the same time I became aware of a noise behind me. Turning, I found myself looking into the eyes of Jesus, for at that moment He was being led by His guards from the judgment hall where He had been examined, across the courtyard to the guard room where He was to be imprisoned for the rest of the night. He had heard my words, as well as the crowing of the cock, and was looking straight at me.

How shall I say what was in that look of His? One of your most gifted Christian poets has interpreted its meaning in lines with which you may be familiar.[1]

The Saviour looked on Peter. Ay, no word,
No gesture of reproach; the heavens serene,
Though heavy with armed justice, did not lean
Their thunders that way; the forsaken Lord
LOOKED *only on the traitor . . . . .*
I think that look of Christ might seem to say . . . .
Did I yesterday wash thy feet, my beloved, that they should
run
Quick to destroy me 'neath the morning sun?
And do thy kisses, like the rest, betray?
The cock crows coldly. Go and manifest
A late contrition, but no bootless fear!

---

1. Quoted by James Stalker (to whom the author gratefully acknowledges his indebtedness) in *The Trial and Death of Jesus*

"I denied Him"

For, when thy final deed is dreariest,
Thou shalt not be denied as I am here;
My voice to God and angels shall attest,
Because I KNOW *this man, let him be clear.*

—E. B. Browning

That look of Jesus was a mirror in which I saw myself. A
few hours before I had vowed that I would go with Him even
to prison and to death. I had proved myself a liar, a deserter,
a traitor, a yellow coward.

But that look of Jesus was also a window through which I
saw His heart! Had there been anger in His eyes, I might
have rushed away to do what Judas did. But there was not a
spark of anger in them! Pain but not indignation! Disappointment and rebuke, but also forgiveness and unutterable
love! In His eyes was a revelation of His heart such as I had
never known. I saw the kind of Master I had denied, and
it broke my heart. It was not my sin alone that made me
weep, but my realization of the kind of Saviour I had sinned
against!

I was not alone at the time. When Jesus turned His head
in my direction, those adversaries of His, who for the time-
being had become my companions, found themselves looking
into His eyes too. They were sinners also, and in desperate
need of cleansing and forgiveness.

Why was I the only one moved to repentance? The answer
to that question is most significant. They had not looked into
the eyes of Jesus before. They had established no earlier relationship with Him. But He and I were friends. Covenant
vows had been spoken between us. We had walked over the
hills of Galilee together until an understanding had grown up
between us such as lovers know. And therefore, like lovers,
we understood the silent as well as the spoken language of
love.

You see, when you come to an hour of temptation which issues in moral failure, it makes all the difference in the world as to whether or not you are already a personal friend of Jesus. If not, when it is all over and you have yielded, all you have left is your sin—the shame and the guilt of it.

But if as a disciple of Christ you happen to fall into sin, then later come to your senses, you find yourself facing not only your sin, but beyond and above it, the searching, loving, forgiving eyes of your Saviour. That is the difference it makes to belong to Him—even though you may sometimes make your bed in hell, you can never get away from His eyes, in which you will always see a love that will not let you go!

That look of His not only melted my heart, it stirred my memory. Instantly I remembered how He had said just a few hours before: "The cock shall not crow this day, before that thou shalt thrice deny that thou knowest me."

But that is not all I remembered, for in addition He had said, "Simon, Simon, behold Satan hath desired to have you, that he might sift you as wheat, but I have prayed for thee that thy faith fail not; and do thou when thou hast turned again, strengthen thy brethren."

You see, He foretold my repentance and restoration as well as my denial, and promised to stand by me all the way through. He had said in effect, "You are going to fail me, but I will not fail you. My prayers will follow you and bring you to repentance. And when you turn back you will find me waiting to forgive you, to restore unto you the joy of my salvation, and to use you again in my service."

And now through the love that shone in His eyes, He seemed to be reminding me of that promise, and reassuring me that His faith in me was not exhausted. Could I assure you that He feels the same way toward you?

Consider for a moment: How many times have you been forgiven? How many times has your soul been restored from wandering? How many times have you been given another chance? And have you reached, you think, the limit of His patience? On the contrary, in His past mercy is your guarantee of His future mercy. He knows that you will sin as well as that you have sinned. He sees the dark hours that are to come as well as those which lie behind, and His forgiving love embraces them all.

"Beyond your next sin," He had said to me, "I will be waiting to forgive you and to restore you. We will make a new beginning, you and I, upon the same old terms. Even though you let me down, I will not let you go." That is the kind of Saviour He was to me, and the kind He offers to be to you—for is He not the same yesterday, today and forever?

And now you understand why, as I "remembered," I was moved to tears. There is a legend to the effect that an angel was once sent to the earth, charged with bringing back to heaven the most precious gift he could find. He searched everywhere and finally returned with a tear of repentance — and that was accepted by God as the most valuable gift earth has to offer.

In his *Divine Comedy* the famous Italian poet Dante tells a story which illustrates the same truth. At the battle of Campaldino in 1289, Buonconte received a mortal wound. By the bank of a stream he lay down to die. God's angel caught him as he sank into unconsciousness. But another spirit, an angel from hell, came swiftly to the place and disputed with the other for his immortal soul. "He is mine," said the Angel of the Pit. "Being the man he was, he is mine by right, and by his own choice." "Not so," said the angel from Heaven," he belongs to me. For he is not what he was throughout life. In the charity of God, he is what he would fain have been as he bethought himself at the end and cried to heaven. See!" said the bright angel, and, opening the eyes of the dead man, they saw the trace of a recent tear!

53

"And must I lose that soul," asks the Angel of the Pit, "for the sake of one miserable tear?"

"Yes," replies the Bright Angel, "for such is the love of God."[1]

And such is the importance of repentance, for while grief alone will not save a man from his sin, there is no hope for him until he does grieve.

But my tears expressed more than grief. Through them I was renouncing my sin and turning from it. More than that, through my tears I was turning back to God. I was giving myself anew to the love I had read in the eyes of Christ, "with full purpose of and endeavor after new obedience."

Repentance, if it is to set a man back on his feet again, must always include taking a new hold upon the hand of God. If it is only sorrow for sin then it is no more than remorse and leaves a man still borne down by his sin. That was the trouble with Judas. He renounced his sin, but he did not re-affirm his faith in Christ. By my tears I did both.

My friend, how is it with you? Have you never shed a tear over your past, viewed in the light of God's mercy revealed in Christ? Doubtless at one time or another you have wept about many things—some of them sad, some of them silly. But has no tear of genuine repentance, leading to newness of life with Christ, ever wet your cheek? Could I, Simon Peter, remind you that it is not sinning that ruins men, but sinning and not repenting! Harden not your heart, I beseech you. Remember:

> *The sacrifice acceptable to God*
> *is a broken spirit.*
> *A broken and contrite heart He*
> *will not despise.*

---

1. For this illustration the author is indebted to Dr. John A. Hutton

"I denied Him"

I pray that my life may be a sermon of hope and encouragement to every one of you. Never yield to despair! You may have sinned grievously and you may have sinned often, but Jesus Christ forgives even unto seventy times seven. Friends may have lost confidence in you, all who know you may despair of you. Perhaps you have little faith in yourself anymore. But I know of One who has not despaired of you. I know of One whose patience is not exhausted. I know of One who is still waiting for you and longing for you—willing to forgive, able to restore. Come!—Come back, or come for the first time, as the case may be, — come to my Saviour and your Saviour and find:

> *Unwearied in forgiveness still,*
> *His heart can only love.*

My soul's response:

> *I could not leave thee, Christ! For when I sought*
> *To fling aside thy counsel, when I thought*
> *That in my crazy freedom I should find*
> *Some way of life for body, soul and mind*
> *Better than thou didst teach, I heard thee say,*
> *'Come back to me, for thou hast lost thy way.*
>
> *I would not leave thee, Christ! For I am lame*
> *From wandering, and the consuming flame*
> *Of passion has gone out and left my soul*
> *A smouldering ember, and the criss-crossed scroll*
> *Of life ends as it started with the line,*
> *'I cannot leave thee, Christ! For I am thine.'*

—*The Disciple*, by Dwight Bradley, in
Quotable Poems, Vol. 1

JOHN

*"I was **His** closest friend"*

*James the son of Zebedee, and John the brother
of James; and he surnamed them, Boanerges,
which is, The sons of thunder.* MARK 3:17

5

"I was His closest friend"
—JOHN

MY NAME IS JOHN, known in the fourth Gospel as "the disciple whom Jesus loved." A common inference from this title
is that I was by nature a lovable character. That, I must confess, was anything but true at the first. Just as the church
has often been too severe with Judas, judging him to have
been a fiend from the beginning, it has often been too kind to
me, judging me to have been a saint from the beginning.

I was anything but a saint on the day that Jesus turned
upon me and my brother James and rebuked us saying: "Ye
know not what manner of spirit ye are of. For the Son of
man is not come to destroy men's lives, but to save them."
(Luke 9:55, 56)

You remember the story. We were passing through Samaria on our way to Jerusalem to keep the Passover. We
needed lodging for the night. Jesus had sent two of His disciples ahead into a village in front of us to make arrange-
ments. As you are aware, Jews and Samaritans held sharp
differences of opinion on certain religious and racial matters
and, in general, had no dealings with one another.

But our Master was different. He lived above prejudice
and bigotry and taught us to do the same. Once before, in
passing through Samaria, He had stopped beside a well to talk
to a sinful woman about the water of life. Not only she but
many of the people from her village believed on Him and wel-
comed Him. So grateful were they for the message of sal-

vation Jesus had brought them that they urged us to abide with them, and we did for two days.

You will recall, also, that Jesus in telling a parable to illustrate what it means to be a true neighbor made the hero of His story a Samaritan. Also, once when He healed ten lepers, one of them—the one who came back to thank Him —was a Samaritan.

The point is—the Samaritans had every reason to treat Jesus and us, His disciples, with courtesy and to extend to us the overnight hospitality which we were asking and for which we were ready to pay. Imagine our astonishment, then, when the two disciples returned from the village to which Jesus had sent them with the report that the Samaritans would not receive us. In the case of my brother and me it was more than astonishment. Our anger blazed forth: "Lord, wilt thou that we command fire to come down from heaven and consume them?"

Little wonder Jesus nicknamed us "Boanerges," which means "Sons of Thunder." It was one of His ways of reminding me that before I could become *Saint* John, the Apostle of *Love,* I had to bring under control my unruly *temper!*

Until I came to know Jesus, I was not unduly concerned about my temper. As is the case with many of your age, I regarded it as a rather minor fault, regrettable, but not a thing to be taken into serious account in evaluating character. But Jesus, as you know, was even more severe with sins of temper than with sins of the flesh.

There is a story concerning a woman of your generation to the effect that she once said to her minister: "I must confess that I explode now and then, but I get over it quickly." To which he replied:: "So does a machine-gun, but it blows everything to pieces." Jesus would agree with that judgment!

There is another story about one of your contemporaries, a young man, who was on a crowded streetcar one morning when he was accidentally shoved by an older man who stumbled as he was getting aboard. The youth flung an angry word at the man and moved on toward the back of the car, without giving him a chance to apologize.

Thirty minutes later, when the same young man entered a business office where he had made application for a position, he found himself in front of the desk of the man to whom he had spoken so rudely on the streetcar a short while before.

"Your recommendations are not bad," said the man behind the desk, "but in view of your lack of self-control on the streetcar this morning, they do not mean a thing to me," And the interview was over!

No, an unruly temper is not an insignificant fault. A combination of jealousy, anger, pride, vindictiveness, cruelty, self-righteousness, touchiness, sullenness, it is one of the worst of sins.

One of the most reputable Christian psychologists of your generation has said: "Enough emphasis has not been put upon anger. It is probable that it is even more destructive of personality, health and happiness than fear." (Ernest M. Ligon)

Anxiety and anger, he holds, because of their disastrous effects upon personality, are the most harmful of all sins. It is not surprising, therefore, to find that in His Sermon on the Mount Jesus had more to say about anxiety and anger than any other phases of human behavior.

But anger is seen to be even more harmful than anxiety when one considers its effects upon society. As an eloquent minister well-known to many of you has written: "No form of vice—not worldliness, not greed of gold, not drunkenness itself—does more to unchristianize society than an evil temper. For embittering life and breaking up communities, for destroying the most sacred relationships, for devastating homes and withering up men and women and taking the bloom of childhood, for sheer gratuitous misery-producing power, this influence stands alone . . .Again and again the Bible returns to condemn temper as one of the most destructive elements in human nature." (Henry Drummond)

Perhaps the reason for this is that ill temper so often is the vice of the virtuous. It is the one blot upon an otherwise noble character. Do not all of you know men and women who are all but perfect except for an easily ruffled, explosive, or touchy disposition? This compatibility of ill temper with high moral character is one of the strangest and most pathetic problems of ethics and religion, but one which can never be reconciled with Christlikeness of spirit.

I am not forgetting that there is such a thing as Christlike anger. Jesus could and did become angry against a public evil such as the legalized system of graft organized and operated by the priests and money changers in the court of the temple. He could and did become angry when He saw wealthy men closing mortgages upon widow's houses and narrow men standing between Him and the healing of an afflicted man on the Sabbath Day, and pretentious hypocrites by their pride and pious platitudes keeping other people out of the Kingdom of God. Jesus' anger, you see, was always social rather than selfish. It was because of and in behalf of others.

But He never became angry because of a wrong done to Him as an individual. "In all such cases, and they were many, He practiced what He preached—going the second mile, turning the other cheek, praying for one's enemies. When they spat upon Him, mocked Him, scourged Him, crucified Him, He did not resent by a single angry word all the public brutality to which He was subjected. 'Who, when he was reviled, reviled not again; when he suffered, threatened not' (I Peter 2:23). He never was angry at a private wrong."

One of your church magazines carried the story of how a Korean Christian conquered his besetting sin. A missionary friend had explained to him that every burst of temper pierced the heart of Jesus. "So I hung a picture of the Lord Jesus on my wall," he said, "and every time I lost my temper I put a thorn on the picture. Soon the picture was almost completely covered with thorns. A great love and shame came over me that He should suffer thus because of my temper, and now He gives me grace in temptation to say, 'Not I but Christ within me,' and His peace comes instead of my bad temper."

My friend, have you learned the secret of conquering that temptation? I, who at the beginning of my relationship with Jesus was a "Son of Thunder," had to learn it, or I had never been known to the world as the "Apostle of Love."

There is another story in the New Testament which reveals how far from saintliness I was at the beginning. It is the one which tells about the day my brother and I came to Jesus with the request, "Master, grant unto us that we may sit, one on thy right hand, and the other on thy left hand, in thy glory" (Mark 10:37). A strange prayer for a saint to offer! You see, at that time I was selfish, greedy, worldly. I was like Judas—interested in Jesus primarily because of the earthly kingdom I expected Him to set up and determined to have one of the chief places in that kingdom.

Before you condemn me, will you not search your own heart to discover just what kingdom you are primarily interested in?

Young people, how is it with you? You live in a land of fabulous material abundance—automobiles, airplanes, jewelry, exquisite clothes, luxurious homes, parties, clubs, movies, sports, television. These are the prizes that glitter before you, and how many are saying: "They shall be mine. I shall pursue them. I shall possess them. I shall be successful, famous, wealthy. This is my aim—to win as many of the world's prizes and to enjoy as many pleasures as I can."

Older men and women, how is it with you? To some extent you have been disillusioned. You perceive, to a degree young people do not yet see, that all that glitters is not gold. Sometimes, weary almost to the point of collapse, you wonder if it is really worthwhile—this "inhuman rat race," this hectic schedule, these high-pressure techniques, this stress and strain to get a little farther ahead—if for no other reason, because everybody else is doing it!

You talk and pray about the Kingdom of God, but it is the kingdoms of this world and the glory of them for which you are striving, is it not?

I speak with great feeling about this, because it was worldly ambition—not drunkenness, not impurity, not godlessness, but greed which brought about the downfall of Judas and which would have ruined me also, John the son of Zebedee, had I not been willing before it was too late to lay my ambition at the feet of Him whom I had come to call Lord and Master.

Looking back upon that day my brother and I asked for those two thrones and realizing how selfish and worldly our request was, I marvel at the patience of Jesus with us. Neither of us ever forgot the searching words with which He closed the interview: "Whosoever will be great among you, shall be your minister: And whosoever of you will be the chiefest, shall be servant of all. For even the Son of man came not to be ministered unto, but to minister, and to give his life a ransom for many" (Mark 10:43-45).

His meaning came home to me with even greater force a few days later. We were gathered in the Upper Room for the Passover Supper, when to our astonishment we saw Him coming with a basin of water and a towel, as though He were a slave, to wash our feet.

He had every human reason to be irritated with us. We had often argued about who was or would be the greatest. None of us was interested in doing the work of a slave. And here He was about to wash our feet! No group of men were ever more completely ashamed or rebuked than we. After Peter's feeble objection, we sat in silence, the silence of humiliation, as He knelt in front of each of us in turn, bathing our feet, then wiping them with the towel.

As He finished He said: "I have given you an example, that ye should do as I have done to you. . . The servant is not greater than his lord. . . If ye know these things, happy are ye if ye do them" (John 13:15-17). In those unforgettable words was the sting of rebuke, but also the healing power of His patience and love.

But the thing that changed me completely was what He said to me from the cross. I was there, as you remember, standing close by as the end drew near, with a few of His devoted followers, among them one dearer to His heart than all the others, His mother—and He committed her to me! "Woman," He said, addressing her and looking upon me, "Behold thy son!" While to me He said, "Behold thy mother!" It was the supreme honor of my life to be entrusted with her care, and from that day forward I provided for her as if she had been my own mother.

Those words of Jesus from the cross made me realize that He loved me as I had never dared to hope, that he had forgiven all my sinning, including my cowardice in running away when He was arrested in the Garden of Gethsemane, and that in spite of my fiery temper and worldliness He believed in me. That was what changed me—His faith in me and His love for me.

My ambition He did not take away, but He did transform it. He transfused it with His own Spirit. He redirected it—

away from self toward service, away from my desires toward His purpose. As you know the eagle has been my symbol down through the centuries. The Master did not turn me into a barnyard fowl; He did not even clip my wings; He only showed me in what direction to fly!

So, as you open the pages of the Book of the Acts, you find that instead of calling down fire from heaven upon the Samaritans, as I once wanted to do, I am preaching to them, laying my hands upon them, and praying that they may receive the Holy Spirit. (Acts 8:15)

Instead of running away from danger or grasping after earthly prizes, I, with Simon Peter, am standing face to face with the same Council which had condemned Christ to death and replying to their command not to speak at all nor teach in the name of Jesus, "Whether it be right in the sight of God to hearken unto you more than unto God, judge ye. For we cannot but speak the things which we have seen and heard" (Acts 4:19,20).

I take no credit for the transformation that had been wrought in me. The power was all in Christ and came to me from Him. I can take credit for only one thing—I had the wisdom to practice staying close to Him. I was one of three with Him on the Mount of the Transfiguration, also one of the same three who waited close by while He prayed in the Garden of Gethsemane. It was I who leaned upon His bosom at the Last Supper. To my shame I fled when He was arrested, but I quickly recovered and found my way into the high priest's house where I stood by Him at His trial. I was at the foot of His cross when He died. Over against my faults and sins, this was my one redeeming trait, and also the secret of my growth in grace and transformation in character—I lived in intimate fellowship with Him. Day after day and hour after hour, I stayed close beside Him.

That is still the secret of transformation into His likeliness. You cannot wish yourself good or even make yourself good. Moral struggle is a painful process and seldom successful. The plan I am recommending is the same as that urged by another first century Christian who wrote: "Let us run with perseverance the race that is set before us, looking to Jesus. . ." (Hebrews 12:1, 2). One of your well-known writers has illustrated what I have in mind by what is to most of you a familiar story—that of a lad by the name of Earnest who gazed so often, always with worshipful reverence, at the Great Stone Face on the mountain across the valley from his home, that his own character grew strong, tender, and kind even as that Face suggested—until at last the people said, "Earnest is himself the likeness of the Great Stone Face."

That was my secret, the secret I was trying to make clear when I wrote the 15th chapter of my Gospel, reminding you that the Christian life at its best is as if Christ were the vine and you the branches; that if you abide in Him and allow Him to abide in you as the branch abides in the vine, then you will naturally, inevitably bear much fruit. So shall you be truly His disciples!

One of your poets has said it in a way that no one could forget:

> *A Persian fable says: One day*
> *A wanderer found a piece of clay*
> *So redolent of sweet perfume*
> *Its odor scented all the room.*

> *"What art thou?" was the quick demand,*
> *"Art thou some gem of Samarcand?*
> *Or spikenard rare in rich disguise,*
> *Or other costly merchandise?"*

"We knew Jesus"

"Nay I am but a piece of clay!"
"Then, whence this wondrous sweetness, pray?"
"Friend, if the secret I disclose,
I have been dwelling with a rose."

—The Persian Fable.

CAIAPHAS

"I condemned Him"

And one of them, named Caiaphas, being the high priest that same year, said unto them. Ye know nothing at all, Nor consider that it is expedient for us, that one man should die for the people, and that the whole nation perish not.

JOHN 11:49, 50

6

"I condemned Him"
—CAIAPHAS

I AM JOSEPH CAIAPHAS, once high priest of the temple at Jerusalem. The office I held was intended to be the highest and the holiest in the nation. As you will recall Aaron, the brother of Moses, was the first high priest. Embroidered in letters of gold upon his blue headdress, were the words "Holiness unto the Lord." Those same words were upon the mitre I wore as I performed my official duties which included entering once a year into the holy of holies where I offered atonement for the sins of the people. Now I realize that it was my sins for which atonement was needed, and for which I made no provision.

It was during the years 18 A. D. to 36 A. D. that I served as high priest. It was I who presided at the meeting of the Jewish council when Jesus of Nazareth stood before us. It was I who said to Him, "I adjure thee by the living God, tell us whether thou be the Christ, the Son of God." When He answered, "Thou hast said: nevertheless I say unto you, Hereafter shall ye see the Son of man sitting on the right hand of power, and coming in the clouds of heaven," it was I who rent my clothes and turning to the other members of the council called upon them to pass sentence immediately. "He hath spoken blasphemy," I said, "What further need have we of witnesses? behold now we have heard this blasphemy. What think ye?" They answered, "He is guilty of

71

death." Then I allowed them to spit in His face, to buffet Him, and to smite Him with their hands.

All this took place at night, which made the trial illegal. Our council, the Sanhedrin was forbidden by Jewish law to hold night meetings. But we were not concerned about legal points so long as we accomplished our purpose to be rid of our troublesome prisoner.

However there was one law we had to respect. The Romans who were our rulers, strictly forbade us to pass a death sentence in any case. So, as early as possible the next morning, I turned Jesus of Nazareth over to Pilate the Roman governor with the urgent request that He be crucified.

In the light of what your New Testament says, and in the light of what I now know, that was a terrible sin. It was blacker than the sin of Judas! He was only a tool in my hand. It was I who paid him the thirty pieces of silver. It was I who laughed in his face when he brought the money back and flung it at my feet with the remorseful cry, "I have sinned in that I have betrayed the innocent blood." The plot was mine—Judas was a minor actor in my play, worth just what I paid him, the price of a slave!

My sin was blacker than the sin of Pontius Pilate! Jesus, Himself passed this judgment upon me when He said, "He that delivered me unto thee hath the greater sin." Pilate found no fault in Jesus. He was kindly disposed toward Him. At heart he wanted to set Him free, but did not have the courage. But I was not kindly disposed toward Him. I was determined that He should die. I delivered Him to Pilate for that very purpose. Pilate, no less than Judas, was a tool in my hand. I despised him as I watched him wash his hands and give orders for Jesus' crucifixion, even as I despised Judas when he took my thirty pieces of silver and went away to betray Him. But both were playing their parts according to my plan.

"I condemned Him"

I had favored and foreseen the death of Jesus long before I was able to bring it about. My reason for desiring it was quite simple, and as I saw it then, quite justifiable. In one of your Gospels is a brief story which makes my point of view very clear. "Then gathered the chief priests and the Pharisees a council, and said, What do we? for this man doeth many miracles. If we let him thus alone, all men will believe on him: and the Romans shall come and take away both our place and nation."

That meeting of our council, known by us as the Sanhedrin, occurred just after Jesus had raised Lazarus of Bethany from the dead—a miracle which greatly enhanced His popularity with the common people. My colleagues, the chief priests and the Pharisees were disturbed no little by His growing influence. They felt that unless we immediately did something to curb His popularity, He might lead an insurrection against Rome and thus bring the wrath of the emperor and his armed legions down upon us.

As you may know, we of the priestly order were working hand in glove with the Roman authorities. By so doing, we were allowed to continue to operate the temple ritual according to our own ideas, which included the collection of a huge amount of graft from our temple bazaars—about that you will hear more presently.

Naturally, for reasons of personal enrichment, we were against any movement or any person who might disturb the *status quo,* so I had a ready solution for the problem created by the popularity of this revolutionary prophet, Jesus of Nazareth. "You act as if you had no knowledge at all," I said to the other members of the council. "Can you not see that it will be expedient for us for this one man to die for the people in order that the whole nation may not perish?"

Leave it to me to always find an *expedient* solution! Jesus, far from being a threat to our security as I saw it,

73

might be used to establish us more firmly with the Roman authorities. By handing Him over to the governor under the charge that He was a revolutionist, we would not only be rid of Him as a troublesome person, but would thereby furnish Pilate with fresh evidence of our fidelity to the empire.

Killing two birds with one stone? Well, not exactly—attaining two ends by one death! The total cost, when my plans were at last complete, thirty pieces of silver. Not a bad bargain from the viewpoint of *expediency!*

It was because I knew the value of *expediency* that I had obtained my office some twelve years earlier. As you may know during the time of the Roman occupation the office of the high priest had become degraded to the point that it was, as you would put it, nothing more than "a political football." High priests obtained and held office, not by virtue of descent from Aaron or by choice of the people, and certainly not by sense of a divine calling, but by appointment from Roman rulers.

In the year 15 A. D., my father-in-law, Annas, was divested of the office because he was "displeasing" to the new governor of Judea, Valerius Gratus by name. In rapid succession the governor tried three others in the office: Ishmael, Eleazer, and Simon. All three failed to "cooperate" as fully as he desired, so in the year 18 A. D. I received the appointment. I must have "pleased" him well, for not only did I hold the office during the remaining eight years of his rule, but was allowed to continue under Pontius Pilate, the next governor. So, you see, by the time Jesus of Nazareth appeared on the scene as my chief problem, I was quite accomplished in the art of *expediency.*

Frankly, I was in no particular hurry to move against Him. I thought it more *expedient* to wait for a favorable opportunity and occasion. I was aware that He had some knowledge of our hostility and also that, at times, He indignantly denounced us for the hypocritical and greedy way we were managing the affairs of our nation. But little did I expect that He would dare to take the offensive against us and challenge our authority. That, as you are aware, is the very thing He did on the morning of what is known to you as Passion Week.

We called it the week of the Passover. It was the most important week of the year to us, not because of its holy associations, but because it was the most profitable for our bazaars. During the Passover season pilgrims came, hundreds upon hundreds, to offer the required sacrifices in the temple. Everyone of them (women, children and slaves excepted) was required to pay the temple tax, the Galilean half shekel, worth between 25 and 50 cents as you value money. On top of this our money changers charged around 20% for exchanging foreign money into the Galilean currency which alone was acceptable to our temple traders who sold the animals required for the sacrifices.

Further, in the temple area we had a complete monopoly on the selling of sheep, oxen and doves, so we charged pretty much what we pleased. The full amount we took in from year to year we kept a closely guarded secret, but it was well known that our coffers were far from empty. It was a good racket—"The Bazaars of the Sons of Annas," and no one had ever dared to challenge the way they were operated— that is, not until that never-to-be-forgotten Monday of Passover Week.

What happened that morning? A well-known writer of your generation has described the incident in the following words:

"To most of the crowd there was nothing unusual in the scene. The air was filthy with the smell of animals and human beings herded together. Men and women trampled one another crying aloud their imprecations. At one side of the court were the pens of the cattle; the dove cages at the other.

In the foreground hard-faced priests and money changers sat behind long tables, exacting the utmost farthing from those who came to buy.

"One would never imagine that this was a place of worship. Yet it was the temple, the center of the religious life of the nation. And to the crowds who jammed its courts, the spectacle seemed perfectly normal. That was the tragedy of it.

"Standing at little apart from the rest, the young man from Nazareth watched in amazement which deepened gradually into anger. His cheeks flushed. A woman's shrill tones pierced His revery like a knife. He turned to see a peasant mother protesting vainly against a ruthless exaction. A money changer with the face of a pig leaned gloatingly over his hoard. . . . The young man picked up a handful of cords from the pavement and half unconsciously now was braiding them into a whip, watching the scene silently.

"Then suddenly without a word of warning, He strode to the table where the fat money changer sat, and hurled it violently across the court. Another step, and a second table was overturned, and another and another. The crowd which had melted back at the start began to catch a glimmering of what was up, and surged forward around the young man. He strode on, looking neither to the right nor left.

"Brushing aside the group of dealers who had taken their stand in front of the cattle pens, He threw down the bars, and drove the bellowing animals out through the crowd into the streets, striking vigorous blows with His little whip. And as His right arm rose, striking its blows, the sleeve dropped back to reveal muscles as hard as iron. No one who watched Him in action had any doubt that He was fully capable of taking care of Himself. No flabby priest or money changer cared to try conclusions with that arm."[1]

---

1. From *The Man Nobody Knows*, by Bruce Barton, copyright 1925, 1952, used by special permission of the publishers, The Bobbs Merrill Co., Inc.

You can imagine the consternation created among us by that act. Far from waiting for us to move against Him, Jesus had walked into our stronghold—into the very place where we thought we had everything under our control, had openly challenged us by driving out our merchants, had even called us a "den of robbers." The nerve of Him! There was too much of the sting of truth in His sharp words for us to wait any longer.

But we had to move with caution. He had a large following among the common people. We did not dare to arrest Him in the open, but we did send some of our colleagues (should I say "henchmen"?) to try to trip Him in His speech so we would have a charge to bring against Him when we delivered Him to the Roman governor. They asked Him, for one question, whether it was lawful to pay taxes to the Roman government. It was a crafty question. Had He answered "Yes," that would have estranged Him from the people, for they were against the Romans and as resentful of "taxation without representation" as some of your forefathers were. Had He said "No," then we could have reported to Pilate that He was preaching revolt against Rome.

Instead He called for a coin—"Whose image and superscription is upon it?" He asked. When someone answered "Caesar's," He said, "Render therefore unto Caesar the things that are Caesar's and unto God the things that are God's!" Astonished at His shrewdness, we gave up trying to catch Him in His speech. But we were still afraid to arrest Him by day —He was too popular. There was just one course left—some subtle plan under the cover of darkness and a trumped up charge to Pilate.

The rest of the story is familiar to you—the bargain with Judas, the midnight arrest, the trial before the Sanhedrin in the darkness of the early morning hours. All of which, as I have already admitted, was strictly illegal. Our law as embodied in the Talmud specifically says, "Let a capital offense be tried during the day, but suspend it at night." Further, Hebrew law provided that no prisoner could be forced to testify against himself. Therefore my effort to question Jesus, as well as that of my father-in-law, Annas, was entirely illegal. One of your writers has found forty-three specific violations of law in His arrest, trial and execution.

What of it? Have I not confessed from the beginning that my actions were always governed by *expedienecy?* Principles such as legality, truth, and right were quite secondary to me. I used them at times, whenever it was *expedient* to do so. At other times, in the name of the same principle, *expediency,* I forgot them.

And I succeeded, did I not? Expediency is truly a wonderful policy if success is one's main aim! Have none of you ever found it *expedient* to cheat on an examination paper? *Expedient* to exaggerate the quality of a product you desire to sell? *Expedient* to cut corners in completing a shady business transaction? *Expedient* to tell a white lie in order to extricate yourself from an embarassing situation? *Expedient,* at your social gatherings, to trim your sails to the winds of popularity, instead of steering a straight course according to the compass of your conscience? *Expedient* to attend church occasionally and to support it niggardly rather than to give it your full heart's devotion? *Expedient* to postpone from week to week, possibly from year to year, your personal commitment to the person and program of Him whom you have come to call, The Lord Jesus Christ?

Am I, Caiaphas, a man apart from you, or are you bone of my bone and flesh of my flesh? *Expediency*—"The subordination of moral principles for the sake of attaining a desired end," who of you does not know the meaning of the word? And what it gets you?

Yes, I, Joseph Caiaphas, found it *expedient* to strike a bargain with Judas, to arrest Jesus by night, to try Him by night, to pronounce Him guilty of death, to trump up a new charge against Him when I delivered Him to Pilate; *expedient* to see Him march to Calvary with His cross upon His shoulders; *expedient* to see Him hanging there until He was dead, dead, dead!

Expediency is indeed a very workable philosophy, if it is the things of this life that you are after. The week after the crucifixion the Bazaars of the Sons of Annas were operating as usual, the silver and gold again pouring into our coffers. So, I, Caiaphas, lived and died a wealthy man.

That was long, long ago, so long that it doesn't seem to matter any more—the silver and gold, I mean.

What does matter, as I see it from today? Just this: The day I condemmed Him to death, though I knew it not at the time, He became God's High Priest in my stead! One of your New Testament writers, the author of the Epistle to the Hebrews, makes this very clear when he writes: "For such a high priest became us, holy, guileless, undefiled, separated from sinners, and made higher than the heavens; who needeth not daily, like those high priests, to offer up sacrifices first for his own sins and then for the sins of the people: For this he did once for all when he offered up himself. Wherefore also, he is able to save to the uttermost them that draw near unto God through him, seeing he ever liveth to make intercession for them" (Hebrews 7:25, 26, 27. ASV).

Wonderful words: words of life and hope and opportunity for every one of you!

Strange, is it not, that I, Joseph Caiaphas, should be saying these things? But you see, while I was upon the earth I never was high priest except in name only. I never tried to save another man's soul. I did not even bother about my own soul's salvation. It was not *expedient* so to do. But, in the place where I now have my abode, *expediency* is no longer a workable principle!

Of this I warn you lest you make my mistake and come to my place of torment.

PILATE

"I sentenced Him"

What then shall I do with Jesus who is called
Christ? MATTHEW 27:22

7

"I sentenced Him"*
—PILATE

I AM PONTIUS PILATE. I have come back to you from the
dead. I shall tell you my story. It may save you from making it your own. Thus I may suffer a little less from the
hell I have made in my own soul.

I was a Roman governor during the time that Tiberias
Caesar was emperor. Rome was then mistress of the world.
The province over which I ruled was known as Judea and I
was governor for ten years. During this time I sat in judgment upon many cases, but am known to the world because
of one. It is of this that I shall tell you.

You know the blot upon my name, the shame I have borne,
lo these 2000 years. But do you know the motives which led
me to my disgrace? Perhaps you will be a little less severe in
your judgment, and find yourself not so different from me if
I tell you the inward workings of my mind on the day I
asked the question, "What shall I do with Jesus who is called
Christ?" How it rings in my ears even yet—that is part of
my hell—then answered it by washing my hands.

Have you ever had a conviction, but refused to follow it?
It was thus that I fell into the abyss from which I have come
back to speak to you today. I knew a certain course was right.
I chose another. There were reasons, of course, good reasons,
it seemed to me then—my popularity with the people, my
standing with Caesar, my desire to get along in the world,
good reasons, yes! But what are good reasons, the best excuses in the world—what are these worth to me now? If

* From *On Toward the Goal* by John Calvin Reid. Used by permission John Knox Press.

you are a lover of excuses, enjoy them while you may, for yet a few years—ah, it may be less than that—they will haunt you night and day and only add to your remorse.

"What then shall I do with Jesus who is called Christ?" This was the question about which I had a conviction. I knew what I should do. But before you pass judgment upon me, remember I knew it not a whit better that you know what you should do! Strange as it may seem, He is facing you today no less truly that He faced me. "Every one that is of the truth heareth my voice." He said it to me, but the words ring in your ears also. My wife had a dream. She pled with me to do the right thing. You have a wife, a mother, a child—some loved one—who has pled with you with no less tenderness and anxiety. Thus far we are all alike. "What then shall I do with Jesus who is called Christ?" We all KNOW what we should do. Where some of us differ is in what we actually do do. As for myself I tried three courses. These mark the downward steps of my shame.

First I tried to EVADE the question.

Those Jewish rulers, how I abhorred them! Coming so early to my palace door. Then refusing to enter lest they be defiled by being in the house of a Gentile on the day of the Passover, all the while clamoring for a man's blood. Straining out the gnat, gulping down the camel! Fastidiously observing the outward forms and ceremonies of their religion, but omitting the weightier matters of the law, such as justice, mercy and faith. Whited sepulchers — outwardly correct and clean, inwardly full of corruption and wickedness! Being a pagan, I was always much more impressed with an orthodox life than an orthodox creed!

But back to my story. Restraining my disgust, I went out to the crowd. "What accusation bring ye against this man?" I asked, scarcely glancing in His direction. And they supposing that I would take their opinion of the case as final and simply pass the death sentence answered, "If He were not a wrong-doer we would not have delivered Him unto thee." Here I saw my first opportunity to evade. I would just allow them to handle the case. "Take Him yourselves, and judge Him according to your law," I said. But they would not have it so. It was the man's blood they were after, and the Roman law forbade them to pass the death sentence. So they answered, "It is not lawful for us to put any man to death." Thus they insisted that I try the case.

Very soon I made a second effort to evade. Once I had talked with the prisoner, I knew He was innocent. I decided to release Him. I stepped out before them all and announced my decision, "I find no fault in this man." As the crowd roared their disapproval, one of the Jewish rulers standing close by said: "He stirreth up the people, teaching throughout all Judea beginning from Galilee even into this place." Ah, "Galilee"? So the man was from Galilee. Galilee was not under my jurisdiction, but under a ruler named Herod, who happened to be in Jerusalem on that day. How fortunate! Let him try the case. So I sent Him to Herod. I watched the procession move off down the narrow street—the prisoner in chains, guarded by my soldiers, the raving mob at His heels. Then I re-entered the palace with a sigh of relief. But it was not all relief. Somehow my conscience was like a boiling sea.

It must have been about an hour later that I heard the shouts of the mob again. From my window I saw them coming back, and their prisoner with them. My plan had failed. Herod was sending Him back to me.

Suddenly a new idea came to mind. It had been customary to release one prisoner at Passover time to please the Jews. I decided to pick out the worst criminal in the whole prison—that Barabbas fellow would be the one, a rebel and a murderer, and to place him beside Jesus of Nazareth and let them decide which one should go free. They would surely choose Jesus. So I thought. What a spectacle they made—

the scowling Barabbas beside the serene figure of the Naz-
arene. "Whom will you that I release unto you," I said,
"Barabbas or Jesus which is called Christ?" Their answer!!!
Who would have believed it? "Barabbas, Barabbas, release
unto us Barabbas, let Jesus be crucified!" O, how long will
men defend dishonor and sin, and crucify nobility and purity? How long will the world cry, "Give us Barabbas—
money, selfishness, pleasure, personal gain, our own way—
Let Jesus be crucified!"

Thus it was that my third effort to evade failed. I have come
back from the dead today to warn you against the folly of
trying to sidestep this question, "What shall I do with Jesus
who is called Christ?" It cannot be done. You may think it
can—so did I, but it can not. There are some questions in
life that force an answer. Refuse to decide them yourself,
and the relentless march of time will decide them for you.
As a young person, you may be unable to decide whether or
not to go to college. You are weighing considerations, you
cannot make up your mind. But the clock does not stop for
your debate; and soon or late at the fork of the road you will
go one way or the other, either to college, or not to college.
Your own mind may not force your decision, but life will.

Or suppose you are in a rowboat, floating down a river.
You are debating in your mind whether or not to stop at a
village three miles below. Continue then your debate, weigh
all considerations, but in the meantime the river has not waited for the conclusion of your argument. In a short while, if
you have not decided the question, the river will have decided it for you. You will not have stopped at the village.

Even so, faith is a forced decision. Debate about it a little
longer, and there will be no debate to it. "You can not escape
the truth. Either you must obey it, and it will lead you; or
you must disobey it, and it will hang on your neck with the
weight of a chain which you will drag forever." "What must
I do with Jesus who is called Christ?" You will evade that

question? Answer it neither way? Try it! Tomorrow, next
week, in a few years at best, it will have been decided for
you, and decided in such a way that the one appropriate symbol for your tombstone will be not a cross, and certainly not
a crown, but a question mark!

*The second course I tried with reference to this question
was to* COMPROMISE. *This part of my story is most difficult,
for here my disgrace is deepest, but to warn you, I will continue.*

I had examined the prisoner and found no fault in Him,
I had sent Him to Herod, and his judgment agreed with
mine. This I told the Jews, and then I added, "I will therefore"—therefore what? You would have expected me to say,
"I will therefore dismiss Him from the bar acquitted, and I
will protect Him, if need be, with the swords of my legions."
Would to God I had said that! But what did I say? How can
I bear to tell it? "I will therefore chastise Him and release
Him." I proposed a compromise. I offered to give Him a
whipping as a sop to their rage, then let Him go, and call it
justice! It was a half-way course, but I thought it would
work.

I sent Him inside. By my order He was stripped to the
waist and a prison guard with a heavy leather whip laid forty
stripes upon His back. Then several soldiers platted a crown
of thorns and in mockery pressed it upon His brow. Blood
trickled down His forehead. Others put on Him a purple robe,
hailed Him as King, struck Him, and spit on Him. Then the
soldiers led Him out. He could hardly stand upon His feet,
after the ordeal to which He had been subjected. I went in
front and shouted to the crowd, "Behold I bring Him out to
you, Behold the man." How pathetic He was—like an up-
rooted flower under the noonday sun! Surely now their rage
will be satisfied, I thought; hate will give way to pity. They
will say, "It is enough" and go home. But what did I hear?

A chorus of voices shouting "Crucify Him, crucify Him." Thus my effort to compromise also failed. Still the question confronted me, "What shall I do with Jesus who is called Christ?"

But it is not the thought of my failure which weighs most heavily upon me now. It is the realization of what a cheap attitude I took. "I can not condemn Him; I will not champion Him. I will straddle the issue, take a middle course, I will release Him with a whipping." I am told that my spirit still walks abroad among men and women of your generation— that there are thousands who are not openly against Jesus of Nazareth, while at the same time they are too selfish or cowardly to take a definite stand for Him. They say, "O, no, I would not deny Him, I believe in Him," yet they do not confess Him. They give Him fair words, but do not open the door; they give Him space in their show window, but not inside their lives. They are neither for nor against, simply trying to sit comfortably upon the fence, halting between two opinions, but making a decision in neither direction.

Compromisers, hear me! If I had my life to live over again, I would either confess Him like a man, or condemn Him like a man! Many sins stained my soul in life, but I was at my worst when I said, "I will *scourge* Him, and *release* Him," the half-way course! The remorse in my soul is ten times more painful because I was a compromiser. Beware, Beware!!

My third mistake was to try to TRANSFER *the responsibility.*

When I saw the worst was coming, I called for a basin of water. I washed my hands before the crowd and said, "I am innocent of the blood of this just person, see ye to it." They accepted my excuse, answering, "His blood be on us and on our children," but that did not take it off me. Blood, blood, blood! I see it everywhere I look! I washed my hands when

I should have exerted them. Blood does not come off so easily. "Out red spot, Out, I say! Here's the smell of blood still! All the perfumes of Arabia will not sweeten this hand of mine, Oh, Oh, Oh!"

O learn today, learn from me, men and women, you can not escape the responsibility for what you are and for what you do. There are those of your age, I understand, who try to place the blame upon environment, the conditions of life in the midst of which they live; or upon heredity, the instincts and tendencies handed down through birth. Yet everyone knows—as I know—that over and above these is the fact of personal responsibility. If a man murders your child, or violates the sanctity of your home, you do not say, "environment, heredity" and let it go at that. One may not be responsible for the conditions in which he lives, nor for all the tendencies in his inner self, but he is responsible for what he does with them. He can say the blame is somewhere else but that does not make it so. He may wash his hands, as I did, but that does not remove the stains. Every man must give account of himself to God.

"What then shall I do with Jesus who is called Christ?" Can you wash your hands of that question? Yes, of course you can! I did. I still do! O God, will I never be able to stop? Must I wash them through all eternity? Transfer the responsibility, does that plan work? Too well! Rub, rub, rub—it keeps on working—wash, wash, wash, but the spots are still there! This inescapable, unchangeable sense of guilt —could this be hell?

Hear this last thing, for my time is nearly spent. My place is calling me back. It all happened in *one day*. All this has come to me because of *one decision*. You are accustomed to measure life by days, and months, and years. That is the way to measure *time*. Life should be measured by crises and decisions. It is quite possible for a man to live more in one day than in the next ten years. One decision may be more important than all the rest of life put together.

You may not know it at the time; I did not. As governor of Judea, I had handed down many decisions. How was I to know my eternal destiny was hanging upon this *one*? *Hundreds* of questions among the Jews I had settled. How was I to know that this, "What shall I do with Jesus who is called Christ?" was the question, beside which all others were as nothing? Yet it was so. How much of life may be concentrated around a single decision! One wrong answer may ruin everything; one right answer may save everything.

The shades are calling! I must away! I must go back to wash my hands some more, and more and more, and evermore! I have testified lest you come to my place of torment. Will you not be persuaded, though one rise from the dead? Remember it all happened in *one* day. To just *one* question I gave the wrong answer—and that question? "What shall I do with Jesus, who is called Christ?"

> *Once to every man and nation comes the moment to decide;*
> *In the strife of Truth and falsehood, for the good or evil side;*
> *Some great cause, God's new Messiah, offering each the bloom or blight,*
> *Parts the goats upon the left hand, and the sheep upon the right;*
> *And the choice goes by forever, 'twixt that darkness, and that light.*

What then will *you* do with Jesus who is called Christ?

SIMON

"I carried His cross"

*And they compel one passing by, Simon of Cy-
rene, coming from the country, the father of Alex-
ander and Rufus, to go with them, that he might
bear his cross.*   MARK 15:21 ASV

8

"I carried His cross"
—SIMON

YOU, PERCHANCE, HAVE KNOWN a day that began bright
with promise and hope—the birds were singing, the sun was
shining, God was in His heaven, all was right with your world
—then suddenly everything changed. Unforeseen and un-
wanted, tragedy appeared, a load was thrust upon your
shoulders which you could not refuse. Black clouds shut out
the light of the sun. But later, looking back, you found that
the clouds you thought dark have become radiant with meaning, the events you called tragic are now seen to be God's
gracious providences, the burden you were forced to carry
has taken to itself wings which now carry you.

If such has ever been your experience, you should be interested in my story. The New Testament introduces me as
Simon of Cyrene. Cyrene, in the first century, was a great city
in northern Africa not far from where the city of Bengazi is
now located. It was there that I lived with my wife and
two sons, all of us devout adherents to the Jewish faith.
Probably some of you are very casual in your attitude toward
the worship services of your church. I thought enough of
the God whom I served to travel more than one thousand
miles to celebrate the Passover Festival in our temple at Jerusalem.

That is how I happened to meet Jesus of Nazareth. At
the time I had no interest in Him whatsoever. In fact we

were going in opposite directions. I was forced to turn around and to go in His direction. That may help you to understand what your theology books call "conversion." The literal meaning of the word is, "a turning around." To be converted, then, means to turn *away from* the direction of your own desires and purposes, and *in the direction* toward which Christ is going. I was forced to make that choice.

I was also forced to carry His cross. That I deeply resented at the first. As I approached the city on that glorious morning, my heart was singing with David, "I was glad when they said unto me, Let us go into the house of the Lord." It was not yet nine o'clock. I intended to be at the temple early so as to miss none of the inspiring services associated with the Passover celebration.

My happy anticipation was rudely interrupted. Just outside the city gate I met a procession headed by three condemned men, each carrying a heavy cross and being prodded along by a band of Roman soldiers. Two were coarse and profane, but the other was strikingly different. There was a nobility about His face that caught my attention at once, and His eyes were expressive of a tender patience such as I had never seen. I could tell He had been horribly abused. A crown of thorns encircled His brow. Caked streaks of blood stained His pale unshaven cheeks. The back of His robe was ghastly red. His hands trembled as they clutched His cross, and as He came opposite me He staggered and stumbled. Instinctively I reached out to support the cross and to help Him to His feet.

Where were His kindred and friends? It seemed strange that no one was ready to help Him. Stranger still since, as I learned later, He had healed hundreds who were crippled or sick. And where were His disciples? I was told later that He had "Twelve Good Men and True" who had sworn never to forsake Him. As I surveyed the crowd for a friend who might carry His cross, one of the soldiers seized my shoulder and commanded me to carry it.

I resented the brusque impertinence of the soldier, representing, as he did, the haughty authority of the Romans, those self-elected lords of creation who spoke to us and treated us as if we were cattle. Did he perchance pick on me because my skin was black from the African sun? Even more I resented his humiliating command. This instrument of death was as revolting to me as it would be to you to handle a hangman's rope. More so, in fact, because it was the Passover season, and this would make me ceremonially unclean. Was I to become a jest for these Roman soldiers, their laughing stock as we walked on toward the place of execution? To passers-by it would look as though I myself were one of the condemned men. Of course, I resented that cross!

In every generation, it seems, people have found reasons to react very much as I did toward carrying the cross of Christ. To take up His cross involves a limitation of personal liberty, self-denial, burden-bearing, sacrifice—the very opposite of self-expression and self-fulfillment. No disciple has ever, at the first, rejoiced to hear the Master's words, 'Whosoever will come after me, let him deny himself, and take up his cross, and follow me." (Mark 8:34).

So it comes to pass that many in your generation also turn away from His cross. Thousands want His salvation, His forgiveness, His friendship, His peace, the social and business advantages of being members of His church, the earthly and the heavenly benefits of His redeeming work, but few indeed are seeking to enter into the fellowship of His sufferings.

And His cross can be avoided. That is one striking difference between you and me. I was forced to carry it. You are not. You have a choice.

What is it to bear the cross of Christ? There are those who speak as though their daily toil, the stress and cares of life, their physical afflictions, the dark sorrows of their bereavements, the strain of caring for an invalid relative—as if these were crosses. Such trials of course can and should be borne bravely in the name and to the glory of Christ, but, properly speaking, such trials are *burdens,* rather than *crosses.* Burdens are universal. They are common to all men and can not be escaped.

But for you and your generation the cross can be escaped. "Many men and women never bear the cross of Christ at all. Many can refuse it if they will, and many do refuse. There are lives of men and women soft-lapped in luxury, which have been lived out from the cradle to the grave and have never known the cross. And there are obscure and unknown men and women who have controlled their lives with such care and prudence and watchfulness and worldly wisdom that they were never tempted to take up the cross. They *live* out their lives in a soft self-pleasing."[1]

For you to bear the cross of Christ involves voluntary sacrifice in either confessing or serving Christ. To make a courageous stand, because you are a Christian, and then to take the consequences of scorn or loss without complaint or pride —that is to bear the cross of Christ. To sacrifice your comfort and time in an earnest effort to win another to His cause, even though you meet coldness and rebuff—that is to bear the cross of Christ. To give sacrificially of your money and service to promote His kingdom at home or abroad, perchance to give your son or daughter or your own life to the cause of foreign missions—that is to bear His cross. To identify yourself with righteous causes or with persecuted people because you believe they are on Christ's side, at the cost of ridicule and reproach to yourself—that is to bear His cross. Cross-bearing, properly speaking, always involves doing something *personal*

1. *The Cross in Christian Experience,* W. M. Clow, page 234

for Christ at a *personal* cost to yourself, and by your own choice.

A well-known minister of your generation has illustrated the meaning of a cross-bearing by telling the story of Subrahmanyam, a young student in India who heard the call of Christ one night while attending a Methodist mission church in Madras. Subrahmanyam came from a Brahmin family, his father was the head of the Brahmin community. When he reported to his father what had happened, one might say that the whole village blazed up in anger. To try to make him change his mind, they tied him to a pillar in the courtyard of their house, stripped his turban from his head—which is itself a mark of indignity in the East—lashed his back with whips until the blood ran, and left him standing hour after hour through the burning noontide. They even had the contents of the sewage can poured over his head. To his grave he will carry two horrible scars, one on either cheek, where his tormentors burned his face with red hot irons, threatening to put out his eyes.

When these men had done their worst and had gone off to the temple, Subrahmanyam's sister slipped out and cut his bonds and he escaped to the hills. In due time, he prepared himself for the Christian ministry and became one of the best known and most highly honored Methodist ministers in all India.[1]

What a far cry from a story such as that to the comfortable life represented by the average church member in America today—too far, I fear, too far!

Another minister of your day complains that Christianity has lost its power because you have made it too easy. You never fast; you do not believe in self-discipline; seldom if ever do you give to the point of sacrifice; you are never ridiculed

1. *Personalities of The Passion* — Weatherhead

97

for your faith, because you live the same way the world lives. You may be interested in the crown of Christ, hardly in His cross.[2]

If what this minister writes is true, then what I am about to say is something your generation sorely needs to hear. While I *resented* the cross at first I changed my mind later. Looking back upon the incident from today, what I thought was my shame has become my glory. Do you sometimes envy those who were privileged to minister to Jesus in His last hours? Mary and Martha who gave Him lodging? The woman who anointed His head with the precious ointment? The "goodman of the house" who provided the Upper Room for the Last Supper? The women who worshipped at the foot of the cross? John who comforted His mother? Joseph of Arimathaea who gave Him a tomb? Nicodemus who anointed His body for burial? None of these deeds can compare with mine. In the merciful lovingkindness of God, it was given to me to carry His cross to Calvary.

The honor had been enough—but I received a twofold reward in addition. Christ, you will remember, never allowed any service done or any honor shown to Him to pass unrewarded. When a village girl asked Him to her wedding feast, He turned the water into wine. When a humble home offered Him hospitality on the Sabbath Day, He touched its mistress, and expelled her fever. When a Samaritan gave Him a drink from her pitcher, He gave her to drink of the Living Water. When a distressed, sinful woman stooped to kiss His feet, He sent her away with His blessing of peace. No cup of cold water given to Him ever lost its reward.

And my reward? First, the salvation of my soul. For from that day I became His disciple. The way He thanked me for carrying His cross made the burden easy and light. The tender way He looked at me made me vow I would spend the

2. O. P. Kretzman — *Voices of The Passion*, page 65

rest of my life in His service. You will not be surprised when
I tell you I stayed there beside the cross to the end. I couldn't
leave Him, not after walking up the hill beside Him. And
when he said to the robber, "Today shalt thou be with me in
Paradise," He turned and looked at me, as much to say,
"I go to prepare a place for you too, Simon, that where I am
you may be also."

But that is not all. I had a second reward. Back in Cyrene
my two young sons were waiting. Everywhere I went I carried their names graven in my heart. So, when I knelt at the
cross I prayed that they might come to know this Friend as
their divine Saviour too. That prayer was not denied me.
Back home some days later, when those two boys climbed upon my knee and asked for a story, I had one to tell them, the
most wonderful story in all the world. And they believed it.
More than that, they opened their hearts to its meaning and
became His disciples too. In their young manhood our family moved to Rome where they became leading members of the
Christian church which by that time had been established
there. That explains why Mark, who wrote his Gospel primarily for the church in Rome, mentions them by name, Al-
exander and Rufus, and identifies them as my sons. That
was my second reward—I lived to see my sons known and
loved and honored in the Church of Christ.

There are few earthly joys which compare to that—the joy
that parents feel when they see their children walking in the
truth. So many parents do not know that joy because their
children fail to hear the old, old story from their lips and
never see Christ's cross on their shoulders.

Are you still hesitating to take up His cross? No one better
than I could understand why you should seek all kinds of
reasons for avoiding it. At the beginning, it was a bitter experience for me too.

But now I see, and would have you see, that carrying His
cross was the crowning adventure, the highest privilege of my

life. To have been allowed to give my strength to the fainting
Saviour, to remove the burden from His bleeding and smarting back—nothing that I ever did can compare to that!

For you, too, a day is coming when any service you have
done for Christ will be the memory of which you will be the
most proud. It will not be the recollection of the prizes you
have won, the pleasures you have enjoyed, the discomforts
you have escaped, that will come back to you with delight as
you review life from its close. But, if you have denied yourself and borne the cross for Christ's sake, the memory of that
will be a pillow soft and satisfying for your dying head. In
that day you shall wish that the minutes given to Christ's service had been hours; and the hours years; and the dollars
hundreds; and every cup of cold water and every word of
sympathy and every act of self-denial will be so pleasant to remember that you shall wish they had been multiplied a thou-
sandfold.[1]

> *Simon of Cyrene bore*
> *The cross of Jesus; nothing more.*
> *His name is never heard again,*
> *Nor honored by historic pen;*
> *Not on the pedestal of fame*
> *His image courts the loud acclaim.*
> *Simon of Cyrene bore*
> *The cross of Jesus; nothing more.*
>
> *And yet, when all our work is done,*
> *And golden beams the western sun*
> *Upon a life of wealth and fame—*
> *A thousand echoes ring the name—*
> *Perhaps our hearts will humbly pray*
> *"Good Master, let the record say,*
> *Upon the page divine, 'He bore*
> *The cross of Jesus,' nothing more."* —Anonymous

---

1. This paragraph paraphrased from Stalker's *Trial and Death of
Jesus*

THE ROBBER WHO REPENTED

"I was crucified with Him"

And he said unto Jesus, Lord, remember me when thou comest into thy kingdom. And Jesus said unto him, Verily, I say unto thee, Today shalt thou be with me in paradise. LUKE 23:42, 43

9

"I was crucified with Him"
—THE ROBBER WHO REPENTED

WHAT AN HONORABLE THING IT IS TO BEAR ONE'S CROSS! But, No! Not always. I carried mine, all the way to Calvary, walking in the footsteps of Jesus of Nazareth. But there was nothing noble or heroic about that deed of mine, because the cross I was bearing was a cross of guilt. It was a cross over which might have been written, "The wages of sin is death." I want to tell you about that cross, to warn you against it, to point you to another which has power to deliver instead of to destroy you.

When did I begin to sin? I cannot remember—even as you cannot recall your first sin. But this I know, it began with *little* things. In every case, the corruption of the human soul is a gradual process. As one of your greatest writers has put it:

> *We are not worse at once. The course of evil*
> *Begins so slowly and with such slight source*
> *An infant's hand may stem the breach with clay.*
> *But let the stream grow wider, and philosophy,*
> *Aye, and Religion too, may strive in vain*
> *To stem the headlong current.*

I sinned in my home, at school, at play, before I ever committed a crime against the state. After my first crime I was frightened. But I managed to escape being caught. So I

103

soon forgot my fright and committed another. I got by once, twice, three times — I could do it again! Thus, step by step, I went from bad to worse.

All my deeds I justified in the name of *personal liberty*. I said to myself, "Should I not be free to do as I please? What right do parents, teachers, rabbis, officers of the law have to tell me what to do? Is my life not my own? I shall do as I wish and go after the prizes I see glittering in front of me.

It all caught up with me in the end. Sin has a way of doing that still—"Whatsover a man soweth that shall he also reap." Not tomorrow, perhaps or even next week, but eventually the harvest has to be gathered in. And blessed is the man who believes this before he has to learn it by bitter experience. I learned it the hard way! That is why I am warning you. Justice does not balance her books at the close of every day, but in due time they are balanced! You may get by for many days. I did, but in the end, "Be sure your sin will find you out."

The wheels of God grind slowly,
But they grind exceedingly small.

When did I realize this? Not until I was dying! With a flash of blinding tearing pain it all came home to me as the nails were driven through my quivering hands, on into the wooden beam of my cross. I saw the shame, the folly, the futility of my sinful years. I saw the man I might have been had I remembered my Creator in the days of my youth.

But I was not yet through my sinning. Two others were being crucified with me. One was my companion in crime. We had sinned together; together we had been apprehended; together we had been condemned; together we were being executed; together we heaped profane and defiant words upon the Roman soldiers charged with our execution.

But no word of reproach or bitterness escaped the lips of the third prisoner. He had been horribly abused. From the crown of thorns upon His head, drops of blood had trickled down upon His forehead and cheeks. As He was being stripped for the crucifixion, great red stripes were visible upon His back where the Roman cat-o-nine-tails had been laid. And yet He was as serene as if He had come into the world for this very hour.

My companion and I resented His composure—just as sin always resents goodness. Also, in our base way we resented the attention He was receiving. The chief priests and scribes who had followed Him to Calvary were heaping ridicule and insults upon Him in which the people joined with mocking laughter, leaving us practically unnoticed. He was stealing the show!

So, although I am now almost too ashamed to tell it, my companion and I joined in the mockery and hurled our reproaches upon Him too. That was my last sin—and, as I now see it, my worst—to cast ridicule and reproach upon Him who died upon that central cross.

Rebuked by His goodness, His patience, His purity, His nobility, I should have prayed. I should have repented. I did later, but first I mocked Him, I ridiculed Him, I reviled Him, I scorned Him. By His mercy I was *pardoned*. By that same mercy, I entreat you never to engage in the sin of speaking irreverently of His person or His cause.

But in due time my profane lips grew silent, and I was moved to pray, rather than curse. What was it that wrought the change within me?

For one thing, I was afraid. All the way to Calvary my companion and I answered the jeers of the people who lined the roadside with scowls and curses. Brazenly we had lived, brazenly we would die! But it was all a front! No man whose life is not right with God is unafraid of death. As I hung there upon the cross with my strength ebbing away, I knew that death would indeed be a dark valley for me, if I had to make the journey alone. At that moment my soul knew a shuddering dread such as I had never felt before.

I was also influenced by the things I heard the crowd say about the third man who was dying with us. Above His head on the central cross was an inscription, "Jesu Nazarenus, Idaeorum Rex." The inscription was there by Pilate's order. That was his way of showing his contempt for the Jewish rulers—"Jesus of Nazareth, king of the Jews." Those who read it laughed scornfully, quoting it to others, adding remarks of derision such as: "He saved others; himself he cannot save," "Let the Christ, the King of Israel, now come down from the cross that we may see and believe," "He trusteth in God; let him deliver him now, if he desireth him, for he said, I am the Son of God."

Could there be truth behind this mockery? I asked myself. After all, who was this man and why did they say these things about Him? Could He possibly be—but that would be too good to be true!

Then I began to think upon what my own eyes and ears were witnessing concerning Him. His patience—"being reviled He reviled not"; His innocence—it was written upon His face and in His eyes; His magnanimity—as the nails were driven into His hands He prayed, not for Himself, not for vengeance upon His enemies—that would have been the kind of prayer I would have offered had I been able to pray at all—but for their forgiveness, "Father, forgive them, for they know not what they do." How incredible! What a strange man!

Could He be more than man? One thing at least was clear, He had done nothing amiss! By contrast I thought of myself. What a base sinner I was! I had no reason to object to my cross. I was receiving the due reward of my sins. My deeds had not seemed so vile as long as I compared myself with others. Until I looked upon Jesus I might have said; "I am no worse than my companion in crime, dying here beside me; no worse than these Romans whose swords are forever cutting into human flesh; no worse than that white-haired old hypocrite of a priest, grown rich by bribery and graft."

But when I looked into the face of Jesus, I had nothing to say for myself, no excuse to offer. I could only confess that I deserved all I was getting and more. You see, it makes all the difference in the world whether one judges himself by others, or in the light of the goodness seen in His face.

There was something about Him that made me hopeful as well as penitent. I found myself yearning for the peace which He so clearly possessed and even faintly believing that I might have it, if I only asked Him. Somehow He made me feel not only that I was a shameful sinner, but that it was possible for me to be saved. That is why I prayed to Him. It was in response to a power which I could feel, although I could not understand it, a power which humbled me and at the same time lifted me up!

The most remarkable thing about my prayer was His answer. He might have rebuked me for the shame of my "deathbed" repentance, He might have reminded me that only a few moments before, I had been cursing Him. He might have said: "My pain is too great, I can not bother with you now." He might have said: "Pray not to me; I am a man like yourself and know as little about the unknown country into which we are both about to enter as you do." Such are the things He might have said had He been no more than man. But He accepted my prayer as if He had the right to hear it and the power to answer it. He spoke of the unseen world as no strange land but as a place native and familiar. He gave me to understand in His answer that in that other kingdom He was King. Great sinner that I was, I laid on Him the weight of my soul, the weight of my guilt, the weight of my eternal salvation, and He accepted the burden willingly— almost joyfully. It amazed me at the time that my burden could be His delight. But I understand now. Since He, as He once said, came into the world to seek and to save the lost, it was natural that my prayer should warm His heart, reassuring Him, as it did, that even at death's door He was still the world's Redeemer and had power to save even unto the uttermost one like myself, who turned to God through Him.

"This," your great Reformer, Martin Luther, has written, "was for Christ a comfort like that supplied by the angel in the garden." God did not allow His son, the Saviour of the World, to come home without bringing one soul with Him— my soul—as a trophy and symbol of His redemptive power.

You, no doubt, at times, have known the testing of faith that goes with unanswered prayer; also the comfort that follows answered prayer. But have you not known also, at other times, the joy of over-answered prayer? Such was my experience when I prayed, "Lord, remember me when thou comest into thy kingdom," and He answered, "Today shalt thou be with me in paradise."

I asked for a blessing in the indefinite future. He answered, *"Today."* I asked for a place in what I thought was to be an earthly kingdom. He promised me a place in His heavenly kingdom, the Paradise of God. I was thinking of some humble insignificant place, He said, "You will be with me." That was the most comforting word of all concerning the eternity which we were about to enter—I was to be with Him. It is still, for you as well as for me, the most comforting of all promises concerning heaven. Where He is, nothing can be amiss. In His fellowship no need is left unsupplied. This is what He meant when He said to His disciples, as your New Testament records, "If it were not so, I would have told you." This is what David meant when He sang: "The Lord is my

"I was crucified with Him"

Shepherd, I shall not want . . . I shall dwell in the house of the Lord forever." No words of mine can tell you just how far His answer surpassed my asking, for eye hath not seen, nor ear heard, neither hath it entered into the heart of man the things which God hath prepared for those that love Him. Suffice it to say that we who met at Calvary's cross-roads, went on beyond the sunset into a new and eternal morning.

Have you ever wondered how it came about that Jesus had to die between two criminals? In so far as the arrangement was man's doing, there was malice behind the deed. Either it was done by order of Pilate to add to the seeming irony of the inscription over His cross, or it was at the request of the Jewish rulers who persuaded the Roman soldiers to give Him this place as an additional insult.

But there was divine purpose behind the wrath of man. As a symbol of the eternal and never-failing mercy of God, between us was His right position. All along His enemies had called Him "a friend of publicans and sinners," and now by crucifying Him with a robber on either side, they put the same idea into dramatic tableau. To all subsequent generations of men it has signified this: Jesus came into the world to save sinners. He identified Himself with them. Their cause was His, and He wrapped up His fate with theirs. He lived among them, He proved Himself over and over their Friend and Saviour, and it was meant that He should die among them. To this day He is still among them, willing and eager to save; but able to save only those who turn to Him in repentance and faith.

This leads to a significant observation about my companion. Why did he not repent too? I urged him to do so. He was just as near that central cross as I was. He too witnessed the

109

quiet dignity of Jesus in the face of death. He too heard Him pray, "Father forgive them for they know not what they do." He knew the end was near. More than that, he heard my prayer and Jesus' wonderful answer. He saw that I had been saved and had entered into peace. Why did he not seek salvation too?

It was not because he was beyond hope, but because he was beyond repenting. His habits had hardened, his attitudes were set, his moral impulses were inert. He no longer felt even a desire to lift up his eyes unto the hills from whence would have come his help. He was alive physically, but already spiritually dead.

Such is the power of sin! Such is the peril of delay. He was so near to the kingdom, yet so far—within nine words of salvation—my prayer was only nine words—but his lips did not move in prayer. Dying right beside the Saviour of the world, still he stepped out into eternity alone! What a perilous thing it is to dally with sin and to delay repentance! One deathbed repentance has been recorded in the Book you know as the Word of God, mine. One that no man may *despair!* Only one that no man may *presume!*

"Today shalt thou be with me in Paradise"—Jesus said. Thus He dropped His still dews of quietness and bade all my strivings cease, and even my disordered life confessed the beauty of His peace. I pray to God that the same Saviour shall one day speak those words to you, and that the same everlasting doors He opened for me will swing wide to welcome you into His heavenly home. And that experience will be yours, I am sure, if you will humbly entrust yourself to His mercy, as did I—for if He could and did save me, He can save unto the uttermost all who turn to God through Him.

110

"I was crucified with Him"

The story of my salvation is proof that no sin is too black, no number too many! So:

Come to the light, 'Tis shining for thee; . . .
Today, if you do hear His voice, Harden not your heart.

My soul's response:

Saviour, I hear, I believe, I come.
Thy arms will strengthen me; and I know
That somehow I shall follow when you go
To the still land beyond the Evening Star
Where everlasting hills and valleys are,
And evil shall not hurt me anymore,
And terror shall be past, and grief and war.

NICODEMUS

"I assisted at His burial"

*And there came also Nicodemus, which at the first
came to Jesus by night, and brought a mixture of
myrrh and aloes, about an hundred pound weight.*

JOHN 19:39

10

"I assisted at His burial"
—NICODEMUS

MY NAME IS NICODEMUS. During the early part of the
first century I was a well known and highly respected rabbi in
the city of Jerusalem. In the Gospel according to John, I am
called, "The man who came to Jesus by night." It is a title
of which I am by no means proud. It suggests that I was at
heart a coward, that whatever my interest in Jesus, I preferred
to keep it a secret.

But I was not altogether a coward. I did not avoid Jesus.
I did seek Him out. Nor did I wait for a special invitation.
I took the initiative. I made the appointment.

In my day and age, as in yours, almost everyone had heard
of Jesus. Some hated and opposed Him; some loved and followed Him. But the majority were just not interested. My
friends, the leaders of the Jews, knew what a stir He was
creating among the common people. Reports had reached
them that He was healing the lame and the blind, claiming
authority to forgive sins and that multitudes were flocking to
Him to hear His teaching. But they were not interested, being
too satisfied with their traditional opinions to do anything
more than to talk about Him, always in either a critical or
condescending manner.

Is it not even so in your day? Are there not thousands who
read articles and books about Him, who have heard countless

sermons, who frequently discuss in academic fashion various aspects of the Christian faith without ever coming to terms with it themselves?

In all Jerusalem, I was the only rabbi to go to the trouble of seeking a personal interview with Jesus. Already, I trust, I am stirring some of you to a sense of personal shame. For I am reminding you that it is ever so much easier to discuss Jesus than to decide for Him, to talk about Him than to enlist in His cause.

Full well I know the excuses which influence a man to refrain from going that far. I was an older man than Jesus. I was much better educated. I was wealthy; He was poor. My family and friends moved in the best circles of society in Jerusalem. Jesus was a peasant from Galilee; His friends were fisher-folk and servants. I was a member of the Sanhedrin, the Supreme Court of the Jews. Why should a man of my standing give Jesus a second thought?

Excuses? I had plenty and to spare, had I been looking for them. Nevertheless, I sought Him out and went to see Him. I have never regretted that I did.

That is why I plead with you so earnestly to listen, not to your excuses, but to your conscience. Is there some longing away down in the depths of your being that has never been satisfied, an unrelieved hunger, a thirst unquenched? Then you need what I needed and what I sought—a personal interview with Jesus Christ!

There are those who postpone coming to Jesus, until trouble drives them to their knees. I was not one of those. I sought no personal favors. In my home was no afflicted son for Him to heal. No personal anxiety was burdening my heart. It was not trouble that brought me to Jesus but my hunger for truth.

Even in my student days, as I prepared to become a rabbi, my mind had been greatly stimulated by the prophets of the Old Testament. One of my teachers, Gamaliel, was among the greatest rabbis of all time. But the more I studied, the more I wanted to know. In particular, I yearned to know more about God—to know the ultimate about Him, the highest truth concerning His nature and His ways with men. That is why I sought an interview with Jesus. I was persuaded that He knew God.

Once I was in His presence, He made me feel that He knew me also and did not intend to waste time on impersonal generalities. Frankly, that was not according to my plan. My intention was to keep the conversation upon the academic plane. I opened the interview by saying: "Rabbi, we know that you are a teacher come from God"—I was trying to be casual, speaking as though I had been sent as a representative rabbi from the Jerusalem School, as a professor from the theological seminary. I was seeking truth, but I wanted it stated in philosophical terms, such as I could use in my lectures or in conversation with my intellectual friends.

But Jesus was thrusting straight at my heart when He replied: "Truly, truly, I say unto you, unless one is born anew, he cannot see the kingdom of God." It was as if He had said, "Nicodemus, let us begin with your personal situation. It is not a Teacher you need, but a Saviour—*you* must be born anew."

That was too direct for me. It was not my condition I had come to discuss. I parried with a question, "How can a man be born again when he is old?"

He knew I was evading the issue. We rabbis were well acquainted with the doctrine of the New Birth. We expounded it daily as a requirement for entering the kingdom of God—only we regarded ourselves, being "the children of Abraham," as already in. It was outsiders—Gentiles, publicans, and sinners—who, according to our teaching, had to be born again. And here was Jesus saying, in effect, that even I, a leading teacher in Israel, needed a new birth.

He had me "on the spot," so to speak, and quite an uncomfortable spot it was at the time. But now I see it was just where I needed to be. I needed to see, as perhaps some of you need to see, that truth becomes *powerful* only when it is received as *personal*. I had come to Jesus upon an intellectual quest. He reminded me that my basic need, as I now believe is the case with every man, was moral. My primary need was in the heart, not the mind. "Nicodemus," He said to me in effect, "let us get away from generalities. Let us be personal rather than philosophical. Let us settle your own problems before we endeavor to settle theoretical problems of theology; and let us settle your most important problem first, the matter of your own salvation. You yourself must be born again."

I am eternally grateful that He refused to allow me to evade that issue. Just as I hope that you, eventually if not now, will thank me for making you face up to the same issue.

I felt increasingly uncomfortable as Jesus persisted in uncovering my personal need by His penetrating psychoanalysis. I had come to talk with the young doctor, not to take His medicine. "I do not need to be born again," I kept trying to assure myself, "but if I do need it, what would I have to do?" Even as I was thinking the question, Jesus answered it by saying: "For God so loved the world, that he gave his only begotten Son, that whosoever believeth in him, should not perish but have everlasting life" (John 3:16).

Was it that simple? The new birth, God's work, not mine; His work of grace following my act of faith in believing in Jesus and in becoming His disciple? Jesus had spoken the words very quietly as if He meant them to be a personal invitation. It was as if He had said: "This is the way you may be born again, Nicodemus. This is the divine plan for your personal regeneration. You can settle the matter right now. This is my invitation." I felt myself drawn to Him as by a magnet.

I was upon the verge of saying, "Lord I do believe; help thou mine unbelief." Then I remembered! What would my friends say? To become an avowed disciple of Jesus, would it not mean ridicule for me, criticism, dismissal from my position as a member of the Sanhedrin? How prudent I had been to come by night. No one need ever know about my visit. The same shadows that hid me from the eyes of men on my trip over were waiting to conceal me as I returned. Blessed darkness! I rose to leave, making some excuse about the lateness of the hour.

Again He read my thoughts. I began to wonder if anything was hidden from Him. In silence He walked with me to the door. Then, laying His hand upon my shoulder (there was a lamp in His other hand), He said ever so quietly: "Everyone who does evil hates the light, and does not come to the light, lest his deeds should be exposed. But he who does what is true comes to the light, that it may be clearly seen that his deeds have been wrought in God."

Those were His last words to me that night. Sharper than a two-edged sword, they found my heart. As I went over the hill, I turned and looked back. He was still standing in the door, the lamp in His hand. All the way home His last words haunted me. I seemed to see walking beside me those two men that had leaped full-grown from His creative imagination: the lover of darkness who avoids the light, and the lover of truth who comes to the light; the moral coward, and the moral hero.

All the while conscience was saying, "The first of those men is you, Nicodemus. The other is the man you want to be, struggling to become you, the man you could and would be if you would only break through your fears and declare yourself openly as a follower of Jesus."

Do you understand that struggle which was going on within me? Is my experience a mirror, perchance, in which you see a reflection of your own soul? If so, I plead with you not to procrastinate, not to postpone your decision—as I did, until shame all but made a mockery of my final heroism.

It was not until He was dying that I came out in the open for Him. There was one earlier time when I almost did. It was several weeks after my night interview with Him. Official opposition to Him was growing, but all the while He was becoming more popular with the people. One day the chief priests and Pharisees sent certain armed officers to arrest Him. They returned without Him, giving as their excuse, "No man ever spoke like this man!" One member of our Sanhedrin hotly demanded: "Are you led astray, you also? Have any of the authorities or of the Pharisees believed in him?" I wanted to cry out, "Yes, I do. I visited with Him one night. What these men say is true. He is the greatest teacher that ever lived. I believe He is more. He is the divine Saviour of the world." Would to God I had said that. Would that I had declared myself as His disciple then and there, regardless of what they might have said or done.

But I was still too much the coward. All I managed to get past my lips was the weak protest, "Does our law judge a man without first giving him a hearing, and learning what he does?" Turning his scornful eyes upon me, the proud Pharisee, who had just rebuked the officers for their failure to arrest Jesus, withered me with, "Are you from Galilee, too? Search and you will see that no prophet is to arise from Galilee." I withdrew into my shell of silence. The coward had won again!

A few weeks later Jesus was upon the cross. That was the event that changed everything for me, His crucifixion! Strange that it should affect me so! Yet not so strange as I think of what that same event has done for countless thousands since.

My memory of the scene is as fresh as though it happened only yesterday—His hands outstretched upon the cross, quiet fortitude in His face, the light of forgiving love in His eyes.

A friend of mine was standing at my side, by name Joseph of Arimathaea. Like myself he was a secret believer in Jesus and, also like myself, a member of the Sanhedrin. But neither of us had attended the illegal meeting the night before at which Jesus had been condemned. Horrified when we heard that He had been sentenced to death, we had hurried to Calvary as fast as we could.

As I gazed up into His face I could see the end was near. Then suddenly it flashed upon me—what He meant that first night when He said to me: As Moses lifted up the serpent in the wilderness, so must the Son of man be lifted up, that whoever believes in him may have eternal life." And, miracle of miracles, the "coward" in me died and the "hero" in my soul took over.

The thing had happened which He was talking about when He said to me, "You must be born again." In that instant, and by the power which flowed from His crucified form into my heart, I became a new man, a man of decision and action. I felt, as one of your greatest hymns expresses it:

> *Were the whole realm of nature mine,*
> *That were a present far too small;*
> *Love so amazing, so divine,*
> *Demands my soul, my life, my all.*

My friend Joseph felt the same way. Then and there we agreed that nothing mattered anymore except our devotion to Him! From then on we would be secret followers no longer— we wanted all the world to know we believed in Him, loved Him, intended to serve Him, were ready, if need be, to die for Him. That explains what we did next. We hurried away to make preparation for His burial—Joseph to secure permission of Pilate that we might take away His body; I to purchase the spices and white linen cloths.

When we returned to Calvary, the evening shadows had lengthened and He was already dead. Hundreds of people were still milling around the scene, among them a number of the chief priests and Pharisees. There were jeers of ridicule and scorn as we prepared to loosen the nails and to take down His body. Somehow we did not mind. They might do and say their worst—dismiss us from the Sanhedrin, drive us from Jerusalem, stone us, even crucify us—we did not care. Our only concern was to render to Him one last deed of mercy as a token of our devotion.

Close by was a garden where Joseph had recently purchased a new tomb, intending that it should be his own. It was to this tomb that we carried Him. Tenderly we washed away the blood from His hands and side and feet; then wrapped His body in layer upon layer of the new linen cloths I had provided, sprinkling between the layers the fragrant spices I had bought. Having finished our sacramental task, we laid His body to rest inside the tomb, and rolled a great stone to the door.

Certain of your Biblical commentators have called attention to the courageous aspect of what we did, pointing out that we were doing what none of His disciples dared to do—they were in hiding; that we were doing it in the daytime before the eyes of many of His enemies; that we were doing it as members of the Sanhedrin, thereby in effect casting a public vote against their cowardly illegal action in arresting, trying and condemning Him at night.

But as Joseph and I walked homeward in the gathering darkness, it was not of our final courage we were thinking, but of our earlier cowardice, our tardiness, our inexcusable procrastination.

Who knows what we might have done for Him and for His cause, who knows how He might have used us and what He might have accomplished through us, had we only taken our open stand for Him sooner? We had done what we could, but there was so much more we might have done had we not waited until that last dark hour!

These were the things we said to one another, Joseph and I, as we walked homeward side by side in the deepening twilight. Grateful beyond words that we had been privileged to lay His sacred body to rest, we nevertheless found our hearts wrung by one wistful regret: So little and so late!

PAUL

"I was His missionary"

One thing I do, forgetting what lies behind and straining forward to what lies ahead, I press on toward the goal for the prize of the upward call of God in Christ Jesus. PHILIPPIANS 3-13, 14 RSV

11

"I was His missionary"
—PAUL

HOW SHALL I INTRODUCE MYSELF TO YOU? I am a man who had two names. Stranger still, I am a man who lived two lives. How utterly different they were!

In my first life, I was Saul—enemy of Christ, persecutor of the Church. In my second life, I was Paul—crusader for Christ, builder of the Church. After I had become a Christian I preached the Gospel with my whole soul, compassing land and sea to make new converts and to found new churches, driven on and on by an irresistible inner urge: "Woe is unto me, if I preach not the gospel . . . for it is the power of God unto salvation to everyone that believeth."

I find it difficult to understand how Christians of the twentieth century can be so lukewarm about their religion. The Gospel is either true or false. If false, it ought to be exposed as a monstrous lie and stamped out. If true, it ought to be practiced at home and promoted abroad until all men have heard the wondrous story and have responded to its redemptive and transforming power. Either it is the greatest delusion ever foisted upon human minds, or it is the supreme revelation of the heart of God to the sin-burdened souls of men.

In either case, neutrality and indifference are out of place. One should be against Christianity with his whole being, or body, mind and soul for it. Either the cross as a symbol is as cruel as it is false and should be torn to pieces and trampled in the dust, or it is a bloodstained standard under which and for which a man should fight all his days! That is the way I saw it in the first century. That is the way I see it still.

At first I thought Christianity was false. Reared in a devoutly religious home, educated at the feet of Gamaliel, the most famous rabbi of his day, intending myself to be a rabbi, I was an ardent believer in the Jewish faith. The idea proclaimed by the Christians that a crucified man called Jesus had risen from the dead to me was nonsense. That such a person should be looked upon as the Messiah of God was worse than foolishness, it was blasphemy! If this crude superstition could not be laughed off by intelligent men; then it had to be stamped out! Who better than I could lead the campaign?

So, I was altogether in favor of the stoning of Stephen and was present at his execution. In fact it was I who kept the cloaks of his murderers while they hurled the stones against his defenseless bleeding body as he prayed, "Lord, do not hold this sin against them." It was I who personally led the persecution against the church in Jerusalem causing the Christians to flee like frightened sheep into the surrounding countryside. Not content with that, I pursued them, breathing threats and murder against them, even as far as Damascus, one hundred and twenty miles north of Jerusalem.

But I never reached Damascus—that is not as Saul the persecutor. For just outside the city the Jesus whose name I had hated, whose resurrection I had mocked, whose church I had laid waste, struck me down—not by the power of a sword such as I carried at my side, but by the brightness of His glory; not in vengeance and wrath, but in loving mercy; not to destroy me, but to save me; not to cast me aside, but to call me into His service. Behind the light which shone around me that day, blinding my eyes, I heard His voice, "Saul, Saul, why do you persecute me? It hurts you to kick against the goads." In that one sentence He laid bare the struggle which had been going on in my soul and released all my tensions. Slaughtering Christians had not been easy for me. I was no murderer by nature. In a flash I realized that He who could thus read my conscience had the right to rule it. "Lord," I said, "what wilt thou have me to do?"

Such was my conversion experience. Dramatic? Yes. Cataclysmic? Yes. But quite simple and understandable. Not removed as far from your own experience as you may be thinking.

For one thing, it was Christ who sought me, not I Him. I am convinced that is true of everyone. No man is good by nature. At heart all are evil, desiring their own will rather than God's will. In various ways men are led to see the folly of living apart from God, but always they are led. Your hunger for God is, as a matter of fact, God's still small voice within your soul. Reach up your hand to find Him, and lo His hand is already there, "outstretched caressingly."

Personally I would never have been saved had not God taken the initiative. Is it not true also of you? "By grace you have been saved through faith; and this is not of your own doing, it is the gift of God." Even what you call your seeking is a human response to something God has already done. One of your hymn writers has expressed this truth which I came to see so clearly in lines which should be quite familiar to you:

> *I sought the Lord, and afterward I knew*
> *He moved my soul to seek Him, seeking me;*
> *It was not I that found, O Saviour true;*
> *No, I was found of Thee.*
>
> *Thou dids't reach forth Thy hand and mine enfold*
> *I walked and sank not on the storm-vexed sea;*
> *'Twas not so much that I on Thee took hold*
> *As Thou, dear Lord, on me.*

We Knew Jesus

I find, I walk, I love, but O the whole
Of love is but my answer, Lord, to Thee!
For Thou wert long beforehand with my soul;
Always Thou lovedst me.

Another thing about my conversion which may help you
to understand your own Christian experience—everything
was not immediately made plain. When I said to the voice
that spoke to me out of the blinding light, "Lord, what wilt
have me to do?" the only answer I was given was, "Arise, and
go into the city, and it shall be told thee what thou must do."
But when I arrived in the city no further revelation was given
me. For three days I was totally blind, so disturbed in mind
that I did neither eat nor drink. After the three days I was
visited by a kind Christian by the name of Ananias. Through
his prayers my sight was restored and by his hand I was bap-
tized. "Brother Saul," he called me and told me Jesus had
sent him that I might receive my sight and be filled with the
Holy Spirit. My question, "Lord, what wilt thou have me to
do?" he answered by saying: "You will be a witness for Him
to all men of what you have seen and heard."

His words astounded me. I was not prepared to preach.
I tried telling the simple story of my conversion in the syn-
agogues of Damascus. The Jews were furious. They were
ready to do with me as I had done to the Christians. I managed to escape, lowered in a basket over the city wall by night.
I made my way into Arabia. For three years I was in the desert meditating, praying, wondering; working out in my mind
the meaning of what had happened to me; and beyond that,
the significance of the birth of Christ, of His death, of His
resurrection.

Not until after those three quiet years in the wilderness
did I find courage to go to Jerusalem to meet the Apostles and
tell them my story. At first they distrusted me and were
afraid. They did not believe that I was a disciple. But one

disciple by the name of Barnabas believed in my sincerity and persuaded the Apostles to accept me. Then I was allowed to preach in Jerusalem as I had done at Damascus.

You see, it was not overnight that all was made plain concerning God's will for my life. My conversion was sudden, but becoming God's missionary was a process, involving days and nights of inner turmoil and uncertainty, and requiring patience and courage in the face of distrust and opposition.

The lesson for you is one of encouragement and perseverance. Do not expect the sunlight of conversion to banish all clouds and shadows. The law of spiritual guidance for you is the same as it was for me: "Tomorrow's revelation waits upon today's obedience." Then, do not be anxious about tomorrow. You know God's will for today. Give yourself to that! Do not expect tomorrow's light until tomorrow's dawn!

> *Look to this day!*
> *For it is life, the very life of life.*
> *In its brief course lie all the varieties*
> *   and realities of your existence:*
> *The bliss of growth;*
> *The glory of action;*
> *The splendor of beauty;*
> *For yesterday is already a dream, and*
> *   tomorrow is only a vision;*
> *But today, well lived, makes every yesterday*
> *A dream of happiness, and every tomorrow*
> *   a vision of hope.*
> *Look well, therefore to this day!*[1]

And for each day, let this be your prayer.

> *Lead thou me on:*
> *Keep thou my feet;*
> *I do not ask to see the distant scene,*
> *One step enough for me.*

---

1 From the Sanskrit

Another thing about my conversion—it did not deliver me from temptation. There was a sense in which it intensified my inner moral conflict. I have written of this in some detail in the seventh chapter of my Epistle to the Romans.

After I accepted Christ as my Saviour, my sins appeared more sinful than ever to me. This was because I had been given a new conscience, as it were. I found I could no longer compromise even with little sins and keep my inner peace. I saw it was necessary to set a guard over my thoughts and desires as well as over my words and actions. Many times I failed—I did the evil that I hated. I fell short of the good which I loved—but I kept fighting! More sincerely, more earnestly than ever, I strove for moral victory.

From personal experience I therefore speak to new Christians this word of encouragement. Do not expect temptation to disappear immediately upon your acceptance of Christ. A decisive battle has been won, but the war has not! After conversion, as well as before, earnest struggle against evil is necessary, and is a sign of spiritual health. Unawareness that there is an enemy within your soul, is a sign that your conscience is asleep, not that your enemy is dead! And that is the situation to fear. Apathy is a sign that something is wrong. To put it in positive terms: as long as you find it needful to fight and as long as you do fight, you have proof that spiritually you are very much alive!

Therefore, "Be strong in the Lord and in the strength of His might. Put on the whole armor of God, that you may be able to stand against the wiles of the devil . . Stand therefore, having girded your loins with truth, and having put on the breastplate of righteousness . . . above all taking the shield of faith, with which you can quench all the flaming darts of the evil one. And take the helmet of salvation, and the sword of the Spirit, which is the word of God. Pray at all times in the Spirit, with prayer and supplication, keeping alert with all perseverance."

"I was His missionary"

Christian dost thou feel them,
How they work within,
Striving, tempting, luring,
Goading into sin?

Christian, never tremble;
Never be downcast;
Gird thee for the battle;
Thou shalt win at last.

Christian, up and smite them,
Counting gain but loss,
In the strength that cometh
By the holy cross.

Another thing I would have you know—becoming a Christian did not bring me exemption from trial and suffering. I came to know in personal experience the meaning of the words of Jesus: "In the world ye shall have tribulation; but be of good cheer, I have overcome the world."

In particular I was greatly troubled in mind by a physical affliction which I have referred to in my second letter to the church at Corinth as "a thorn in the flesh." This affliction I regarded as a handicap to me in my Christian service. I felt I could do a much more fruitful work as Christ's missionary if I were cured. Three times I prayed to the Lord, earnestly beseeching Him to heal me.

That He did not do. He denied my request, and yet He answered my prayer. I came to see that God always answers true prayer in one of two ways—either by changing the circumstances or by supplying sufficient power to overcome them. In my case He used the second method. He said unto me, "My grace is sufficient for thee: for my strength is made perfect in weakness."

133

After all, what a great answer to any prayer that is! Let me pose a question: Among the people you know, what class do you most respect and admire? Is it those who have found life easy and pleasant with scarcely an obstacle along the way? Is it not rather those who have encountered all kinds of difficulties and handicaps, but who somehow have found within themselves a power more than equal to their trials and who, thorns and all, have been able to say as I learned to say, "I can do all things through Christ who strengtheneth me."

And why is it that you do admire such people? Is it not because you instinctively recognize that they possess the one blessing which, of all God's gifts, matters most; namely His grace in all-sufficient measure.

If you lack that measure of grace, perhaps the reason is that in your praying you are too intent upon the thing you are praying for, and not intent enough upon the God to whom you pray. You have no ears but for the answer you expect. You are tuned in only to the wave length of your personal desires. You pray in the attitude of "no substitutions, please."

Thus you are unable to hear God saying, "I have something other and better for you than the thing which you are seeking." Perhaps He is trying to say that to you this very moment. Give Him the opportunity. Learn to accept, as did I, His substitute answers to your prayers. By so doing you will oftimes receive blessings inconceivably more rewarding than those which you in your limited wisdom had been seeking.

A little poem with which you may be familiar puts it this way:

> *Life's walls imprisoned me.*
> *Shut in with pain and care,*
> *I pined for sunlit air,*
> *The bird's sweet melody.*

"I was His missionary"

Then from my bitter anguish came the cry,
'O God, remove these walls that tower high,
And give me freedom out beneath the sky!

Still stand the walls the same,
God did not give release;
Yet light is mine, and peace—
The gracious Master came.
He came into my dark abode one day
And brought the joy that cannot pass away,
The song that ever in my heart will stay.

Of one thing more I must remind you—my Christian experience involved a commission as well as a conversion. Salvation, I learned, was an experience not to be enjoyed, but to be shared. I was called, not only to be His disciple but to be His missionary. I came to feel that the most important words He spoke after His resurrection were these: "Go therefore and make disciples of all nations, baptizing them in the name of the Father and of the Son and of the Holy Spirit, teaching them to observe all that I have commanded you: and lo, I am with you always, to the close of the age."

Count it not boasting as I summarize my labors and imprisonments for the sake of the Gospel. Five times I received at the hands of the Jews forty lashes, less one. Three times I was beaten with rods; once I was stoned; and three times I was shipwrecked; a night and a day I was adrift at sea; on frequent journeys I encountered dangers from rivers, from robbers, from my own people, from Gentiles—in cities, in the wilderness, upon the sea. Many a sleepless night I spent. I knew hunger and thirst, cold and exposure. I bear on my body literally the marks of the Lord Jesus. In heaven, it has

135

been said, "God will look you over not for medals, but for scars." Have you any scars to show?

No, for you take it too easy—the Christian life, I mean, the Great Commission in particular. In one respect at least your age and mine are strikingly similar. In my day we thought the end of the world was near because we expected the early return of Christ. In your day many think the end is near because of the atom bomb.

But there the similarity ceases.

Because we thought the end was near we preached Christ, calling upon men everywhere to repent, seeking to save as many as we could before the final curtain came down!

And you build battleships, airplanes and bombs! Could it be that the distress of your generation is God's judgment upon you for treating so lightly His divine command to evangelize the world? If Christians of your generation possessed even one half the missionary zeal that the Christians of my generation possessed, then the Kingdom of God might be breaking in upon the world instead of the kingdom of Communism.

Be that as it may, I would to God I might return and live upon the earth once more. For then would I go again to those who have never heard the Gospel, that I might tell them the old, old story of Jesus and His love,—how that love lifted me, how it is still the power of God unto salvation to everyone that believeth! Yes, seeing your self-satisfied generation of American Christians, and across the sea the vast multitudes who do not know your Christ and mine—I have just one regret—that I had only one life to give as His missionary!

LAZARUS

"He raised me from the dead"

And when he thus had spoken, he cried with a loud voice, Lazarus come forth. And he that was dead came forth, bound hand and foot with grave clothes: and his face was bound about with a napkin. Jesus saith unto them, Loose him, and let him go. JOHN 11:43, 44.

12   (An Easter Message)

"He raised me from the dead"
—LAZARUS

I AM LAZARUS OF BETHANY whom Jesus raised from the dead. Mine, therefore, is a fame no other man can claim. Enoch was translated that he should not see death. He "walked with God; and he was not; for God took him." Moses was buried by God's own hand, and "no man knoweth his sepulchre to this day." Elijah was carried by a chariot of fire in a whirlwind to heaven. There was something uniquely miraculous about the final departure of these men, but none of them came back from the realm of the dead to live again upon the earth and to speak of that other land. But I did come back. My body had lain in the tomb for four days when my spirit heard the mighty voice of the Son of God saying, "Lazarus, come forth." And I came forth— still bound hand and foot with grave clothes, nevertheless alive, once more a man among men, walking upon the face of the earth!

You think that a thrilling experience? It was dying that was the thrilling experience! I came back reluctantly. For four days I had lived in heaven. And no one who has feasted upon heaven's joys could wish for earth again.

139

Doubtless you would like to hear from me a detailed description of what I saw—where is heaven? What is it like? Is it an actual city with streets of gold and gates of pearl? You are asking the impossible. Can your dog, for example, comprehend what it means to be a human being? He understands a few words you speak, possibly performs two or three tricks at your command, responds to your deeds of kindness with a wag of his tail—and that is all! When you are reading Tennyson's *Idylls of the King,* or listening to a symphony, or engaging in worship, or enjoying the companionship of your family and friends, you are in a world so far above your dog's world that he does not and can not begin to understand its meaning.

In like manner and for a similar reason, heaven is above and beyond the comprehension of the human mind. If I, Lazarus, were to attempt to describe it, I would have to use the language of heaven, whereas you are able to understand only the language of earth. So, I can only say, as the heavens are higher than the earth, as God's ways are higher than your ways and His thoughts higher than your thoughts—so, higher than the farthest flight of your spiritual imagination, are the glories of that other world.

Jesus was imparting to His disciples this very assurance when He said, "If it were not so—" if even one of your worthy hopes and expectations were doomed to disappointment, if anything were lacking—"I would have told you." Even I, Lazarus of Bethany, brought back by His power, can tell you no more than this: "Eye hath not seen, nor ear heard, neither hath it entered into the heart of man, the things which God hath prepared for those that love Him." Blessed beyond all words are they "that do His commandments, that they may have the right to the tree of life, and may enter in through the gates into the city."

This should help you to understand why He does not call your loved ones back. It is only human that you should long for them—"O for the touch of a vanished hand, and for the sound of a voice that is still!"

> *Beside the dead I knelt for prayer,*
> *And felt a Presence, as I prayed,*
> *"Restore again to life," I said,*
> *"This one who died an hour ago."*

He does not answer such prayers—why? He has the power. Their spirits, as was mine, are not beyond the sound of His voice. Is it because He is lacking in love? No, but because He loves *them* no less than *you!* For their sakes, He denies your prayer. Could you see heaven, for even one brief moment, as I have seen it, you would understand how selfish it is, how unfair to ever wish or pray that a loved one should return.

But if heaven is all that I say it is, why did Jesus call me back? Not for my sake, but for the sake of others. Do you remember it is said, "He groaned in the spirit and was troubled, as He came to the grave"? He was reluctant to call me back, even as I was reluctant to come back. But He did it for the sake of my sisters and for your sakes who also believe, to prove that *there is no death.*

My sisters believed in the resurrection, that in the final day the dead would arise from their graves and enter into heavenly bliss. You remember how Martha said to Jesus, "I know that my brother shall rise again in the resurrection at the last day." But where would I be between death and the resurrection? That was the question that worried my sisters. That was the cause of their deepest grief.

And Jesus told them that there was no dark period of waiting, no purgatory, no soul-sleep, no intermediate state, but in effect, the souls of believers at their death are made perfect in holiness and do immediately pass into glory. You will recall His exact words "I am the resurrection, and the life: he that believeth in me, though he were dead, yet shall he live: and whosoever liveth and believeth in me shall never die." That is what He declared to be the truth about death, and He called me back to prove it! A short time later He gave the same glorious assurance to the robber who was crucified beside Him, *"Today* shalt thou be with me in paradise."

He called me back that those who believed on Him might look once again into my face and never be concerned any more about the resurrection. Whether "resurrection" means that the particles which now constitute your body will actually again come together and form another physical body, or whether your heavenly body will be entirely new and wholly spiritual—what matter the various interpretations and conjectures regarding "the Doctrine of the Resurrection," so long as you hear the voice of your Saviour, the Son of God, echoing down through the centuries—"Whosoever liveth and believeth in me shall never die?"

The Scripture says my tomb was a cave. That is the way it looked to those who buried me. But by coming back I proved it was a tunnel! It had two openings, not one! The same is true of every Christian grave—it is a passageway through the mountain to the Promised Land. A gate and a stairway to the stars! Or, to put it in the language of your generation, to die is to step into the airliner "Salvation," to take your seat behind a Pilot who has made the roundtrip Himself and who can be trusted absolutely, who furthermore is your personal Friend, and to wing your way into the stratosphere beyond which lies God! A fearful prospect? Rather the most thrilling experience that can ever come to a human soul!

"He raised me from the dead"

If I take the wings of the morning
And dwell in the uttermost parts of the sea.
Even there shall thy hand lead me,
And thy right hand shall hold me.

A rather famous play has been written about my resurrection entitled "Lazarus Laughed." The significance of the title and the idea running through the four acts is that I, having discovered that there is no death, find no place in my heart for fear and sorrow. I am done with weeping; I know only laughter.

Thus, in scene two of the first act when a band of Roman soldiers sweeps down upon a group of my friends and relatives gathered in the street, leaving ten mortally wounded, I look upon the scene and with a triumphant smile say to those around me, "There is no death."

A man bending over one body says, "Here is your father, Lazarus. He is dead."

A woman beside another body says, "This is your mother, Lazarus. She is dead."

And still another, "And this is Mary, Lazarus. She is dead."

And I answer, "Yes! Yes!! Yes!!!" each yes more exultant than the former, because I am remembering the new life into which they have entered. Then from the depths of my exultant spirit, I begin to laugh—a quiet, contented laugh swelling to one of triumphant assurance, compelling all who hear me, even the centurion and his soldiers, to join in my laughter and to take up my song:

Laugh! Laugh!
Fear is no more!
There is no death!

143

We Knew Jesus

> *There is only life!*
> *There is only laughter!*
> *Death is dead!*

In the final scene of Act Four, Tiberius Caesar, who because of his guilty conscience cannot endure my laughter, has me bound to a stake over a huge pile of fagots, and orders the fagots lighted. As the flames leap up around my body, he and his soldiers give themselves to mockery:

> *Ha-ha-ha-ha*
> *Burn and laugh!*
> *Laugh now, Lazarus!*
> *Ha-ha-ha-ha!*

For once my voice is unable to respond because they have bound my mouth with a gag. But I laugh at them through my eyes until even Tiberius wants to hear me speak again and orders a soldier to cut away the gag.

Then Tiberius says: "Quick, Lazarus! You will soon be silent! Speak! In the name of man's solitude—his agony of farewell—what is beyond there, Lazarus?"

Forgetting my pain from the fire, I give my ringing answer: "Life! Eternity! Stars and dust! God's Eternal Laughter." And once more my voice breaks forth into exultant, triumphant, expectant laughter![1]

That, according to Eugene O'Neill, is the way I died the second time, by which he suggests that all good men would die with laughter in their eyes and hearts if they only knew what awaits them in God's Eternal Beyond.

In declaring that, O'Neill is only re-echoing the basic message of the New Testament. Only, it seems to me, the New Testament says it still more triumphantly: "Who shall sep-

1. From *Lazarus Laughed*, by Eugene O'Neill, copyright 1927, by Boni & Liveright. Used by special permission of Random House, publisher.

arate us from the love of Christ? Shall tribulation, or distress, or persecution, or famine, or nakedness, or peril, or sword? . . . No, in all these things we are more than conquerors through him who loved us. For I am sure that neither death, nor life, nor angels, nor principalities, nor things present, nor things to come, nor powers, nor height, nor depth, nor anything else in all creation, will be able to separate us from the love of God in Christ Jesus our Lord."

Or again: "When the perishable puts on the imperishable, and the mortal puts on immortality, then shall came to pass the saying that is written: 'Death is swallowed up in victory.' 'O death, where is thy victory? O death, where is thy sting?' . . . But thanks be to God, who gives us the victory through our Lord Jesus Christ."

Thus Paul the Apostle laughed at death. Thus every Christian should laugh on this glad Easter morning—every one whose trust is in Him who stood beside my tomb and said: "Whosoever liveth and believeth in me shall never die."

There was another change wrought in me about which I must speak. After being in heaven for four days, I saw *life* with new eyes as well as *death*. I understood, as you can only begin to understand, that great saying of the Apostle Paul: "The things which are seen are temporal; but the things which are not seen are eternal."

From earliest infancy I had been taught that evil was evil and that I should shun it; that good was good and that I should seek it. In eternity I learned that it is not enough to distinguish between the evil and the good. Almost anyone who has the courage to listen to his conscience can do that. The real test of moral wisdom is to be able to distinguish between the things that pass and the things which abide. Many of the monuments that men build by means of money, ambition, and power are not evil. But they have no value beyond this life; therefore, what folly to make them so important!

Do you recall the story Jesus told about the man concerning whom God said, "Thou fool"? It was not for *wickedness* that he was condemned, but for *shortsightedness*. In his planning and striving he saw no farther than the horizon of earth. He was amazingly successful as his goods increased and his barns expanded. Had he lived in your day he would have been head of one of your great corporations, his safety deposit box bulging with stocks and bonds, envied by multitudes. He had personality, power, success, security—seemingly he had all the answers.

But for one question, as the story reveals, he had no answer whatsoever—"When thy soul is required of thee, these things which thou hast prepared, whose shall they be?" Could you, as was the case with me, have four days in eternity, you would see how true it is, as Jesus' story implies, that of all the fools in the world, the greatest is "he that layeth up treasure for himself, but is not rich toward God."

But there is a way to use the things of earth so that they take to themselves an eternal value. There is a way to handle material things so that you become rich toward God in the process.

As one of your contemporaries has said, if violins are to be the only product, there is little reason why Stradivarius should spend his life making them. The music wooed from their strings by some master violinist lingers for a moment upon the ear, then vanishes upon the waves of the air. A few years, a few centuries at the most, and the violins of Stradivarius, like all human achievements, will be dust and ashes.

But what if the violin is making Stradivarius, all the while he is working upon it, no less truly than that Stradivarius is making the violin? What if *souls are being made or unmade* in the world's workshop, no less truly than machines? What if the most important question with regard to your work is not *what you are doing with it;* but *what is it doing with you?* Integrity, thoroughness, honesty, accuracy, conscientiousness, faithfulness, patience—these qualities which constitute character and complete the soul are woven into it only through *work.* Honest and good work make honesty and goodness in the worker and apart from work these qualities are non-existent.

A well known play of your generation has the significant title, "You Can't Take It With You." There is a sense in which that is profoundly true. The money you make, the houses you build, the transactions you complete, the successes you achieve—these things are related to the earth and upon earth they will remain when you have taken your final departure.

But that is not the whole truth. Money you waste upon earth's baubles and vanities, that you cannot take with you; but money you invest in Christian outreach—in the church, in the education of a worthy boy or girl, in world missions, in humanitarian service—that you do take with you.

Work done for wages only, with your eye on the clock and your mind on your pay check, that you cannot take with you; but work that you do in such a way that day by day you are made more unselfish, cooperative, trustworthy, considerate, skillful, patient, and kind—that kind of work produces something in you—a soul quality which will be with you through all eternity.

Time that you waste in dissipation and sin you cannot take with you, for "nothing unclean shall enter" that city; but time that you spend in wholesome amusement and recreation leaving you refreshed in body, mind, and spirit and thereby a finer man or woman—that you do take with you.

147

Adversity that you accept with bitterness or complaint, that you cannot take with you; but suffering or sorrow borne with Christlike fortitude, thereby producing in you a larger measure of patience, trust, serenity, and consecration—that you do take with you, a part of your expanded immortal soul.

This is what Jesus meant when He said: "Lay up for yourselves treasures in heaven, where neither moth nor rust consumes and where thieves do not break in and steal." To be rich rather than bankrupt when you arrive in heaven you are to exchange your work, your money, your time, even your play for the qualities which constitute character—no other currency will be negotiable on the other side. Thus the things which are "seen" will be translated into the things which are "not seen," and your deeds in time will become investments in eternity.

This, then, is the message I, Lazarus of Bethany, speak to you on this glorious Easter Morning!

Fear not death, for there is no death. For those who truly believe in Him who called me from the grave and said, "He that liveth and believeth in me shall never die," there is only life—part of it on earth, the rest in heaven!

But fear life, lest you waste it, lest you misuse it, lest the earthly portion be gone before you know it, leaving you only land and stocks and bonds which you cannot take with you. For what counts on the other side, and the only thing that counts, is not what a man has, but what a man is!